John Maynard Keynes

Life, Ideas, Legacy

Mark Blaug
Emeritus Professor, University of London
Consultant Professor, University of Buckingham
Visiting Professor, University of Exeter

in association with the
INSTITUTE OF
ECONOMIC AFFAIRS

First published 1990

Published by
THE MACMILLAN PRESS LTD
Houndmills, Basingstoke, Hampshire RG21 2XS
and London
Companies and representatives
throughout the world

Printed in Great Britain by
Billing and Sons Ltd
Worcester

British Library Cataloguing in Publication Data
Blaug, Mark, *1927* —
John Maynard Keynes: life, ideas, legacy.
1. Economics. Theories of Keynes, John Maynard, 1883–
1946
I. Title   II. Institute of Economic Affairs
330.15'6
ISBN 0–333–49652–3 (hardcover)
ISBN 0–333–49653–1 (paperback)

To Ruth

Contents

List of Plates

Preface

In 1988 I wrote and presented a one-hour documentary video film entitled *The Life, Ideas and Legacy of John Maynard Keynes* for the Institute of Economic Affairs, London. This has been well received both by the economics profession and by a wider audience at home and overseas. It went on to win a Silver Medal at the prestigious New York Film and Television Festival, and is available on video cassette for purchase from the IEA's distributor Guild Sound & Vision Ltd, 6 Royce Road, Peterborough, PE1 5YB, England.

In the course of making the programme, I had a unique opportunity of interviewing a number of colleagues and relatives of Keynes, as well as some famous modern economists, including Nobel Laureates, in an effort to assess his legacy. The inevitable time constraints of the medium of film forced me to be extremely selective in making use of these valuable conversations. One of the purposes of this book is therefore to make these interviews available in their entirety. The conversations are permanent records of leading economists 'thinking aloud'; of themselves they are of limited value except in the technical context of the debate about the nature and significance of Keynesian economics, a debate which has now raged for over half a century. It therefore proved necessary to introduce these interviews with some exposition – however preliminary – of Keynesian theory, which is in turn illuminated by a brief consideration of Keynes's life and times. Hence the structure of this book, *Life, Ideas, Legacy*. The book in many respects provides both a permanent record and a scholarly extension of the IEA video. While the book and the video are self-contained, they are mutually reinforcing.

This is a book addressed to the general reader and particularly to beginning students in economics. It presumes no prior knowledge of economics but only a desire to learn something about one of the great social scientists of the twentieth century, whose ideas for good or for ill have probably had a greater impact on economic affairs than that of any other economist in history.

I thank the Directors and staff of the Institute of Economic Affairs for providing me with the opportunity to make the original film. I particularly thank Nigel Maslin, the producer, and all those whom I quote in the book for their co-operation. Their words are their own; the conclusions are mine. I hope I have bridged the gap.

MARK BLAUG

Introduction

Economics is not a subject much given to intellectual revolutions. Two hundred years ago Adam Smith may have wrought a revolution in convincing his contemporaries to place trust in the workings of unregulated markets. A century later a number of economists certainly produced a so-called 'marginal revolution' which turned economists away from a concern with growth and development towards a concern with value and distribution as governed by allocative efficiency. And fifty years ago, the publication of *The General Theory of Employment, Interest and Money* (1936) by John Maynard Keynes produced a Keynesian Revolution in economic thought – that is, the massive conversion of virtually all economists in the Western world to a new style of economic thinking in the unbelievably short period of 4–5 or at most 8–10 years. By the time Keynes died in 1946, Keynesian economics was well on the way to becoming a new orthodoxy, dissension from which characterised one as a crank or fuddy-duddy. For the next 30–35 years, governments everywhere adopted policies recommended by Keynes or at least associated with Keynes's name. In more recent years, such policies have been largely abandoned as mistaken, but many economists continue to support Keynesian prescriptions and to attribute the apparent failure of policy-makers to come to grips with the twin problems of inflation and mass unemployment precisely to the pursuit of anti-Keynesian ideas. In short, the validity or invalidity of Keynesian economics is still a matter of passionate controversy among economists worldwide.

This much would justify an interest in Keynes as a thinker. In addition, however, Keynes provides one of the great examples of the economist as journalist, teacher, university administrator, scholar, editor, statesman, businessman, financial speculator – a sort of Leonardo da Vinci of the social sciences. For the professional economist, he serves as a role model. For the man and woman in the street, he serves as an object lesson of what it takes to be influential in public life. For the student of economics, he continues to remind them that economics as a subject is both very easy and very difficult: it is very easy to see that, faced with the mass unemployment following the Great Depression of the early 1930s, Keynes in opposition to economists of the day had the right answer; it is very difficult to see, however, that an answer that was right in the 1930s may well be wrong in the circumstances of the late twentieth century. Is economics therefore a subject in which there are no absolute truths but only truths relative to time and place? It is this sort of question that makes Keynesian economics both fascinating and important to students of economics.

1 Life

The Keynesian Revolution is a label for the dramatic change that took place within economics in the 1930s with the publication of *The General Theory of Employment, Interest and Money* (1936) by John Maynard Keynes. The Keynesian Revolution is largely the story of the impact of that book, but Keynes had published many books before that one and its appearance capped a long career as economic theorist, economic journalist and economic advisor. It is doubtful whether the same book published by an unknown would have had the same revolutionary influence. In short, Keynes's life in the preceding fifty-odd years before 1936 is of some significance in the bombshell that was *The General Theory*. It is for that reason that we begin a book on Keynesian economics with a brief history of Keynes's life.

He was born in Cambridge in 1883 (the year of the death of Karl Marx), the oldest son of John Neville Keynes – also an economist and author of a still readable book, *The Scope and Method of Political Economy* (1891) – and Florence Ada Keynes, an early graduate of Newnham College, Cambridge, and the city's first woman mayor. In other words, Maynard's family background was prosperous, well educated and solidly middle class. The family resided in a street in Cambridge called Harvey Road, and Maynard Keynes's first biographer, Sir Roy Harrod, argued that his entire life was coloured by what Harrod called 'the presuppositions of Harvey Road' – meaning a Victorian compound of moral earnestness, worldly improvement and rational persuasion by a self-appointed élite. Such was young Maynard's inheritance from his parents.

Keynes was educated at Eton with the aid of a modest scholarship, and this led on in 1902 to a distinguished scholarship in classics and mathematics at King's College, Cambridge. At King's College his interest broadened to literary and philosophical matters, and it was here that he formed the personal friendships that were to last him the rest of his life. He was invited to join the Apostles, a small, secret society of dons and undergraduates who met periodically to discuss ethical, aesthetic and even political questions. Among the younger Apostles were undergraduates like Lytton Strachey, Leonard Woolf, E. M. Forster and Bertrand Russell, who were later to form the core of the artistic group known as the Bloomsbury Group, a tag invented by a journalist to describe the group of Bohemian painters and writers living in and around Bloomsbury, an area in Central London.

Among the older Apostles were philosophers like G. E. Moore, whose *Principia Ethica* (1903) preached an anti-Victorian doctrine of scepticism of conventional values, replacing these instead by a peculiar mixture of 'aesthetic values' and personal relationships as the only meaning in an otherwise meaningless world. Moore provided the Apostles and subsequently the Bloomsbury Group with a tremendous sense of liberation, licensing them to re-examine all traditional standards in terms of purely personal criteria of morality. This was no less important for Lytton Strachey, Forster and Keynes, who were homosexual or bisexual, than for Leonard Woolf, Roger Fry, Clive Bell and Virginia Woolf, whose personal lives were less controversial but whose artistic ideas were outrageous (for example, they welcomed the French post-impressionism of Cézanne and Picasso). In any case, the ideas of G. E. Moore must have reinforced 'the presuppositions of Harvey Road' for the young Keynes, leaving him with an unshakeable sense of confidence in his own judgement about the great issues.

When Keynes graduated in 1905 at the age of 22, he decided to take up a career in the Civil Service. To prepare himself for the entry examinations, he attended lectures on economics at Cambridge by Professor Alfred Marshall and wrote essays for him. He entered the Civil Service in the following year and worked for over two years in the India Office, although he never actually visited India. Out of this work grew his first book in economics, *Indian Currency and Finance* (1913), a descriptive study of the pre-war working of the gold-exchange standard.

Even before he entered the Civil Service, Keynes had started work on a Prize Fellowship Dissertation for King's College on probability theory. He continued to work on the dissertation during office hours in the Civil Service and it gained him a Fellowship at King's in 1909. For the next few years he combined teaching in economics at King's with additional work on the dissertation, which finally appeared after a number of further revisions as *A Treatise on Probability* in 1921. This book, relatively neglected by economists until recently, is well-known among philosophers as a leading example, indeed *the* leading example, of the subjective approach to the logical foundations of probability. It depicted probability as a degree of confidence in rationally held beliefs and not as an objective frequency of occurrence of actual events.

However, by the time he came to publish *A Treatise of Probability*, Keynes had already acquired world fame in a wholly different area. Shortly after the outbreak of the First World War, he took leave of absence from Cambridge to re-enter the Civil Service as part of the regular Treasury staff dealing with the financial side of the war. Here he advanced rapidly to become by 1919 the senior Treasury official in the British delegation to the Peace Conference at Versailles and the official representative of the British Empire on the Supreme Economic Council. Keynes had earlier held pacifist objections to the war, and in the course of the discussions leading up to the Versailles Peace Treaty, he became increasingly disheartened by the harsh terms that were being imposed on Germany. Consequently, he resigned from the British delegation and returned to England to write *The Economic Consequences of the Peace*, a slim book, or rather an extended pamphlet. The book was written at white heat in less than six months and appeared in British bookshops in December 1919. It was an instant, overwhelming success and turned Keynes overnight into a world celebrity. Ever after, his name was familiar to every newspaper reader and radio listener, and whatever he wrote or said was immediately snapped up by the media. There are some modern parallels among economists, for example John Kenneth Galbraith, Milton Friedman and Friedrich Hayek. But even Galbraith, Friedman and Hayek pale in comparison to the popular fame and instant recognition that Keynes achieved with *The Economic Consequences of the Peace*.

Keynes' basic argument in the book was that the Versailles Peace Treaty was a Carthaginian peace, designed not so much to punish as to cripple Germany; that the war reparations imposed on Germany could not and hence would not be paid; and that the economic progress that Europe had experienced before the war had rested on a particular system of international interdependence that had been shattered by the war and that should have been, but was not being, restored by the Treaty. The intellectual arguments of the book were vivified by brilliant pen-portraits of Lloyd George, Clemenceau and Woodrow Wilson, the principal architects of the Versailles Treaty, displaying for the first time the memorable prose style that was to become one of Keynes's hallmarks. The *Economic Consequences* remained throughout the 1920s at the forefront of a continuous debate about German indemnities, and as late as the 1940s it was blamed as being responsible, at least in part, for the appeasement of Hitler by the Allies and hence for the outbreak of the Second World War.

The success of *Economic Consequences* led Keynes to substitute journalism and currency speculation for work in the Civil Service. These activities were eventually to make him a very rich man and

possibly one of the richest economists who has ever lived. His
personal fortune fluctuated from a high in 1924 to a low in 1929 to a
new high in 1936, when he was worth somewhere around half a
million pounds (about ten million pounds in today's money). He still
continued to give a set of lectures for one term in the year at
Cambridge and he took an active part in the life of King's College,
becoming its Bursar in 1924; however, he never returned to his heavy
pre-war load of teaching and supervision in Cambridge. As editor of
the *Economic Journal*, a position he had originally taken up in 1911,
he was naturally in the forefront of all inter-war debates in economics, because then as now the *Economic Journal* was the leading
professional journal of British economics.

In 1923 Keynes published a slim book entitled *A Tract on Monetary
Reform* which marked him out as a leading advocate of what we
would now call 'monetarism' – that is, the doctrine that a government can steer the economy solely by monetary policy. However,
'steering the economy' in the 1920s did not mean then what it means
today: it meant stabilising the level of prices by manipulating the
exchange rate and the rate of interest and not raising or lowering the
level of output and employment variables which were then regarded
as being no part of the business of governments. The *Tract* contained
few theoretical innovations, but its emphasis on positive monetary
management of the economy did mark something of a break from the
Cambridge tradition of Marshall and his successor, Arthur Pigou.

In 1925, Keynes amazed all his old friends by marrying Lydia
Lopokova, a prominent member of the Diaghilev ballet company.
His friends were surprised because Keynes had hitherto shown no
interest in women. Moreover, Lydia spoke little English and went on
speaking 'funny' English for the rest of her long life. Finally, although
she was artistic and interested in theatre as well as ballet, she was
totally alien to the Bloomsbury circle that Keynes had moved in since
his student days. Nevertheless, it proved to be an extremely happy
marriage, and in time Lydia managed to charm all of Keynes's
friends, many of whom confessed in later years that their early
resentment of her melted away with the years. Just after his marriage,
Keynes took a lease on Tilton, a farmhouse near Firle in Sussex,
some fifty miles south of London. Tilton was just down the road from
the country base of the 'Bloomsburies', Charleston Farmhouse,
where Clive Bell, Vanessa Bell and Duncan Grant decorated most of
the rooms, painting walls and even furniture with designs similar to
those that Duncan Grant painted for Keynes's rooms at King's

College. Tilton became the house where Keynes did most of his serious writing in later years, but he also owned a Georgian townhouse in Gordon Square in Bloomsbury where he spent most of the week. The routine that he kept up more or less throughout the remainder of the 1920s and the whole of the 1930s was London from Tuesday to Friday, Cambridge from Saturday to Monday during term-time, and Tilton for the remaining weekends and long vacations.

Keynes made his first trip to Russia with Lydia in 1926. It resulted in a revealing and characteristic pamphlet, *The End of Laissez-Faire* (1926). He revisited Russia in 1928 and 1936 and recorded his impressions on both occasions. It is interesting to see that he avoided both the total condemnation and the uncritical admiration of the Soviet Union that was the standard reaction of so many of his contemporaries. Politically he was now firmly allied to the Liberal Party and particularly Lloyd George's wing of the party. He was a frequent speaker on Liberal platforms, and his brilliant pamphlet *Can Lloyd George Do It?* (1929), co-authored with Hubert Henderson, summed up his defence of the Liberal pledge to conquer unemployment by spending on public works. More than one commentator has noted the extraordinary fact that *The General Theory* really is a book about theory, and that public works to remedy unemployment is a topic that is hardly even mentioned in it. However, we must remember that by 1930 informed opinion in Britain and in the rest of Europe knew that Keynes stood for 'spending one's way out of depression' by road-building, municipal housing construction and the like. Besides, any doubt on that score was settled by another of Keyne's effective pamphlets, which started as three articles in *The Times* in 1933, *The Means to Prosperity*.

Keynes was never satisfied with being just a successful economic journalist or a successful financial speculator. It is clear that he also hankered after the applause of his fellow economists. Throughout the latter half of the 1920s, he was at work on a major *Treatise on Money* that appeared in two volumes in 1930. The book was at first well received, although many of the readers were put off by the 'fundamental equations' set out in pages and pages of extremely tedious algebra. However, a savage review by Hayek and an only slightly less savage review by Dennis Robertson set the tone for an increasing number of hostile criticisms, some of which were the more telling because they were privately communicated to Keynes by colleagues and friends. There are many elements in the book that were to reappear in *The General Theory*, such as the fundamental distinction between investment and saving and their equality or inequality governing the overall level of economic activity, but there are also many others, such as a concern with price stability as an objective of economic policy, that did not survive to the later book. Suffice it to say that by 1932 Keynes, having earlier decided to revise the *Treatise*, had come to feel that what was needed was a completely new book. That new book, *The General Theory*, took longer to write than he could possibly have imagined. It was in fact over four years in the making.

We shall consider the content of that book in the next chapter. Let us, however, tell the story of the rest of his life, a mere ten years. In 1936 Keynes founded the Arts Theatre in Cambridge, partly as an acting venue for Lydia and partly as a touring theatre for the city of Cambridge. He had hoped initially to sell shares in the theatre but ended by financing it entirely himself; it survives as a thriving venture to this day.

In the summer of 1937, after feeling ill for some months, Keynes suffered a severe heart attack. That heart attack marked the end of his contributions to economic theory. The remainder of his life was devoted to problem-solving in applied economics, having to do first with the preparations of war, then with the pursuit of the war itself, and finally the problems of post-war reconstruction. In the event, given his state of health, it was extraordinary how much activity he managed to cram into the last remaining decade of his life.

Keynes continued to edit the *Economic Journal* and to publish articles on economic policy in the pages of *The Times* and elsewhere. When war broke out, he re-entered the Treasury, not as a Civil Servant but, as he himself put it, a 'demi-semi-official' – that is, an unpaid advisor to the Chancellor of the Exchequer. Six months after the outbreak of hostilities, he published his recommendations on war finance, *How To Pay for the War* (1940). Although he details of his proposals for compulsory saving were never accepted, the general principle of paying for the war by deliberately deferred consumption became the foundation of British war finance. Moreover, the 1941 Budget was couched in *The General Theory* language of macroeconomic accounting and so marked the more or less official endorsement of Keynesian economics, a mere five years after the appearance of *The General Theory*.

In the following years Keynes became Lord Keynes or Baron Keynes of Tilton. The remaining war years were filled with endless memoranda to official commissions and inquiries. Having spoken in favour of public subsidies to the performing arts, he became Chairman of the Committee for the Encouragement of Music and the Arts in 1942. Four years later this became the Arts Council, with Keynes once again serving as its first chairman. As the war drew to a close, Keynes became increasingly involved in post-war international economic policy centred around the creation of the International Monetary Fund and the World Bank. He attended the Bretton Woods Conference in 1944 and the Savannah Conference in 1946 as a British representative and presided over a British delegation that visited Washington in 1944 and 1945 on Lend–Lease and the US loan to Britain.

Keynes died at Tilton on 21 April 1946.

Of all the many personal reminiscences of Keynes, my own favourite is that of Clive Bell, the husband of Vanessa Bell, and the brother-in-law of Virginia Woolf. A famous art critic and a central figure within Bloomsbury, it is the more telling in that Clive Bell confessed that he never really liked Keynes:

> In spite of all the little annoying things that have stuck in my memory, my recollection of Maynard, vivid and persistent, is that of a delightful companion. I miss him . . . What I miss is his conversation. It was brilliant: that is an obvious thing to say but it is the right thing. In the highest degree he possessed that ingenuity which turns commonplaces into paradoxes and paradoxes into truisms, which discovers – or invents – similarities and differences, and associates disparate ideas – that gift of amusing and surprising with which very clever people, and only very clever, can by conversation give a peculiar relish to life. He had a witty intellect and a verbal knack. In argument he was bewilderingly quick, and unconventional. His comment on any subject under discussion, even on a subject about which he knew very little, was apt to be so lively an original that one hardly stopped to enquire whether it was just. But in a graver mood, if asked to explain some technical business, which to the amateur seemed incomprehensible almost, he would with good-humoured ease make the matter appear so simple that one knew not whether to be more amazed at his intelligence or one's own stupidity. In moments such as these I felt sure that Maynard was the cleverest man I had ever met; also, at such moments, I sometimes felt, unreasonably no doubt, that he was an artist.

2 The Ideas

The General Theory of Employment, Interest and Money is an exceedingly difficult book, and to this day there is little agreement among economists about its central message, or rather little agreement about the precise specification of the central message, and particularly the route Keynes chose to reach his basic conclusions. The main message of the book is clearly that a modern capitalist economy is constantly plagued by unemployment and that this unemployment is caused by a deficiency of what Keynes called 'aggregate demand', the sum total of spending by consumers and investors. There is a constant danger that there won't be enough total spending to buy back all the output of a fully employed economy; there is a constant threat that some output will go to waste because there is not enough spending to purchase that potential output.

Paradoxically, this problem of the possible deficiency of aggregate demand gets worse as a society becomes more affluent. The more affluent the society, the larger the amount of income people are inclined to save rather than to spend on consumption. This tendency to save more creates no difficulties provided the saving is converted, via the money market, into an equivalent amount of investment spending on factories, plant and equipment, machinery, etc. But if there is not enough investment spending to absorb the increased volume of saving, the result will be unemployment, and of course there is no mechanism that guarantees the conversion of every pound sterling of saving into an equivalent pound sterling of investment.

This is the idea of *The General Theory* in a nutshell, but to understand Keynes's analysis we must briefly explore some of its key concepts. Keynes had long been associated in the public mind as an advocate of public works to remedy unemployment. The theory of public works spending was that workers employed on public works would spend at least some of their earnings on, say, groceries; grocers would in turn spend some of their receipts on ordering more foodstuffs; farmers would therefore get more orders from wholesalers and hence would increase production; increased agricultural production would generate demand for seeds, fertilisers, and so on and so on, through an apparently endless round of subsequent effects, all raising incomes and hence employment throughout the community.

The trouble with this conception was that it was imprecise, because at each round some of the income 'leaked out' in the form of savings and debt repayments; how could one be sure that the stimulating effects of the extra consumption at each round would not be wiped out by these leakages? What Keynes did in *The General Theory* was to give precision to the notion of the multiplied effects of spending on public works by the introduction of the so-called 'consumption function', a new and absolutely central concept in his thinking.

The consumption function says that total consumer expenditure in any given year is a stable and highly predictable fraction of national income; in most economies it is about three-quarters of household income, and it always rises and falls as income rises and falls. Now, this may strike us as a trite and rather obvious idea, but it was in fact only confirmed by data gathered six years after the publication of Keynes's *General Theory*; it was, in short, one of Keynes's bold but accurate empirical conjectures.

The residual of income over and above consumption spending is called 'saving'. On the other hand, investment is something done by business firms. Because saving and investment are done by different people for different reasons there is no guarantee, as we said before, that the two will be the same. What, then, brings them into harmony or, as economists love to say, into equilibrium?

It used to be said before Keynes that it was changes in the rate of interest that performed this function: if savings were plentiful, interest was low, and that made investment plentiful; likewise, if savings were scarce, interest was high and that dried up investment. But instead, Keynes argued, it is variations in income itself that bring savings into equilibrium with investment and, moreover, it is investment that is always the active partner in the relationship; when investment goes up, this causes a multiplied increase in income; that makes consumption go up but never by as much as income rises, and that difference in turn generates the savings to match the initial increase in investment.

What we have here are three or four highly interrelated ideas: the consumption function, the 'multiplier', which we have not yet explained, and a particular set of definitions of savings and investment. Let us look at all these now in just a little more detail.

First, we must think of consumption, investment, saving and income as forming a 'circular flow' in which business firms pay out wages, rents, interest and profits to households in return for the services of labour and property, and households pay out consumption

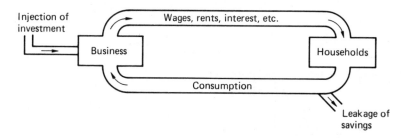

Figure 2.1 The circular flow of purchasing power in the economy

pounds to business in return for goods and services (see Figure 2.1). Business enterprises cannot expect their sales to consumers to be as large as the total of their outgoings on wages, rent and interest because the public will want to save some of its income; these savings therefore 'leak out' of the circular flow. That does not matter provided that businessmen are at the same time 'injecting' a sufficient amount of additional wages, rents and interest payments for new investment goods. The total amount of income flowing around the circular flow will go up when businessmen try to invest more than consumers are saving; vice versa, income will fall when plans to save exceed plans to invest.

We now introduce Keynes's concept of the multiplier to show that any increase in investment will have a multiplied effect on income, and *that it is this increase in income that generates the saving to match the increase in investment.*

Suppose that, for whatever reasons, investment increases by £100 and *that all of this £100 is spent on hiring extra workers.* These workers receive an increase in income of £100 and, according to Keynes's consumption function, there is a stable relationship between extra income and extra consumption; that is to say, every time income goes up by £1, consumption goes up by three-quarters of £1. So, our workers spend £75 of their extra £100 of income to buy groceries, and the grocers spend three-quarters of the £75 they receive on food for themselves and on new orders from their wholesalers, who in turn spend three-quarters of their extra income, leading to an ever-dwindling series of consumption spending and re-spending (see Figure 2.2).

The amazing thing is that this dwindling series does *not* go on for ever: it adds up to a very definite number. If the workers spend 3/4ths of their extra income on consumption, the multiplier would have

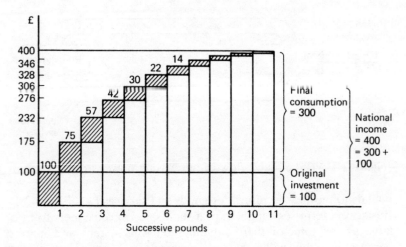

Figure 2.2   The consumption function

been 4; if they had spent 7/8ths, the multiplier would have been 8. In other words, the greater is the community's extra consumption re-spending, the greater is the multiplier effect of investment.

So what? You may say: 'I thought that Keynes was going to show us that public works can cure unemployment and that we can precisely calculate *how much* we need to spend on public works to cure just so much unemployment.' But that is just what we have now done. We kept speaking of increases in investment and let you think that it was *private* investment, but the whole argument works just as well on *public* investment, on money spent by governments on public work programmes. What Keynes is saying is that the expenditure multiplier is always greater than one, which follows from the consumption function, the statistical relationship he discovered between aggregate consumption and aggregate income. If the expenditure multiplier is always greater than one, it must be true that any amount of unemployment can be cured by a sufficiently large increase in public spending. The stimulus of this public spending is larger if it is financed by borrowing, by soaking up idle money rather than by taxation, but even if it is wholly financed by taxation, unemployment is still curable by a sufficiently large amount of public spending.

This is really an extraordinary conclusion. Economists had been debating the likely pros and cons of public works in depressions for over a century without coming to any definite conviction. We have just spent a few pages expounding the simplified Keynesian theory of income determination and have shown that a given amount of public or private spending simply must raise national income by at least as much, and possibly by much more, and in this way is capable of eliminating any amount of unemployment. This is one of the central lessons that Keynes brought to economics.

The stark simplicity of the argument is wonderfully captured by a diagram which Keynes himself never used but which was invented by Paul Samuelson a few years ago for the re-publication of *The General Theory*, to transmit the essence of Keynes's theory to students of economics (Figure 2.3).

If we draw the horizontal and vertical axes of a Cartesian diagram to the same scale, a 45-degree line drawn north-east from the origin

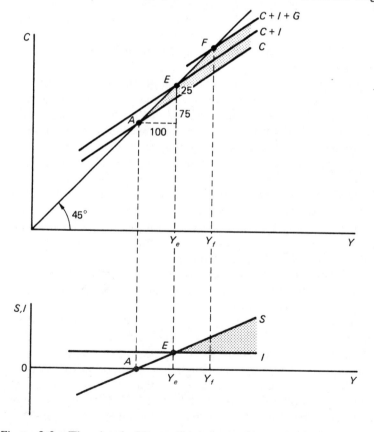

Figure 2.3 The simple Keynesian income theory in diagrammatic form

will have the special property that the distance up from the horizontal axis exactly equals the distance across from the vertical axis. Let us depict national income Y along the horizontal axis and consumption C as a component of national income along the vertical axis; then at any point along the 45-degree line, consumption exactly equals income.

Suppose we are at a 'break-even' point such as A. Keynes tells us not only that consumption is a function of income, that it varies as income varies, but also that it is a particular function of income: as income rises, consumption always rises, but by less than the amount by which income rises. As Keynes put it, the 'marginal propensity to consume', MPC, is always less than one; that is, the fraction of *extra* income that is spent on consumer goods is always less than one. That proposition is expressed by our line C, which has a slope of less than one, the slope of one being the 45-degree line. Previously we said that in modern economies it is typically 3/4th or 75 per cent of national income. In that case, the slope of the consumption function C is as shown in Figure 2.3.

At point A, people consume the whole of income; as income rises beyond A, they consume a smaller and smaller portion of income, which means they save a larger and larger portion of it. In other words, 'saving' is defined by Keynes to be income minus consumption, which implies that the 'marginal propensity to save', MPS, is the mirror image of MPC. If MPC is 3/4, then MPS is 1/4. We can depict the saving function, whose slope is MPS, on a separate diagram underneath the one for the consumption function; in the top diagram saving is the shaded area between consumption and the 45-degree line; in the bottom diagram it is exactly the same area between the horizontal income axis and the savings function, being in fact the flip-over version of the upper diagram.

It is an axiom of Keynesian economics that income is determined by the level of aggregate demand. But aggregate demand is the sum of consumption expenditure, investment expenditure and government expenditure. We have discussed consumption expenditure, but we have not yet said anything about investment expenditure or government expenditure. In order to expound the essence of Keynesian theory, we shall make the simplifying assumption that government expenditures are zero and, likewise, that there are no taxes, no foreign trade, and no undistributed business 'disposable income' available for spending by households or as 'national income' or GNP, because all the factors that distinguish one from the other in national income accounting have been assumed away. However, they can be introduced subsequently without altering the essentials of the argument. That leaves private investment, a key element in Keynesian theory, which cannot be assumed away even in an elementary exposition of the doctrine. Keynes had much to say about the determinants of what he called the 'marginal efficiency of Capital': it depends on the rate of interest, tax policy, current levels of income, expected future income, and business confidence, and it is highly volatile, in marked contrast to the stability of consumption expenditure. We can divide investment into 'induced' and 'autonomous' investment, depending on whether or not it is a function of current income levels. For simplicity's sake, we are going to confine investment to autonomous investment, meaning that investment is whatever it is regardless of income; that is shown by a horizontal line *I* in the lower part of Figure 2.3, or, equally, by the addition of the *I* curve to the *C* curve in the upper part of the figure.

We are now ready to draw the argument to a conclusion. The total consumption and investment spending *C* + *I* curve shows the levels of desired spending by consumer and business firms at each level of income or output. The total spending curve crosses the 45-degree line at point *E* in Figure 2.3. Point *E* represents an equilibrium, because at that level desired spending on consumption and investment exactly equals the level of total output. If output were less than or to the left of point *E*, the *C* + *I* spending would be above the 45-degree line, so that planned spending on consumption and investment would exceed planned output. In that case, shops would run out of goods and business firms would gear up to increase their production; as a result, output would increase and we would move back to point *E*. Contrarily, if output were greater than or to the right of point *E*, the *C* + *I* spending would be below the 45-degree line, so that planned *C* + *I* would fall short of planned output. In that case shops would find that they have too few customers and would find inventories of goods piling up against their wishes. Obviously, the result would be cutbacks in production, so that output would fall, moving the spending back to point *E*. Point *E* is the only level of income or output at which everyone's plans will be satisfied – at which sales, production, employment, spending and income will have no tendency to change – and that is why we rightly call point *E* an equilibrium level of income or output.

This argument was conducted in terms of total spending, the upper part of Figure 2.3. But the same conclusion is reached by focusing on the lower part of the figure, depicting the tendency of the planned saving of households and the desired investment of business firms to be brought into equality by variations in the level of output of income. The only equilibrium level of Y is at E, where the savings function S intersects the investment function I.

So far so good. We have shown that the equilibrium level of national income is determined by the volume of effective demand made up of spending on consumption and investment. The point is, and this was Keynes's punchline, this equilibrium level of income Y_e is not necessarily a full-employment level of income Y_f; indeed, Y_e is typically less than Y_f (see Figure 2.3), and there are no forces in a capitalist economy that automatically bring Y_e into line with Y_f; hence the need for fiscal or monetary policy on the part of government to pull Y_e up to Y_f. For example, if 'autonomous' government spending were added to $C + I$, so that aggregate demand would equal $C + I + G$, point F in Figure 2.3 would represent the equilibrium level of income of such an economy, in which case Y_e would be brought into equality with Y_f. Put simply, there is always some level of government spending capable of producing full employment in any economy whose private spending would otherwise fall short of a full-employment level of income.

We have not yet exhausted the tricks that can be performed with the 45-degree cross diagram of Figure 2.3. We spoke earlier of the pivotal role of the multiplier in Keynes's theory but we seem now to have lost sight of it. However, the multiplier is present in Figure 2.3 and is implied by the very curves we have drawn. Let us recall that the 'multiplier' refers to the amplified effect of investment on output: a unit increase in investment results in a more than a unit increase in output. But how much more? We showed earlier (Figure 2.2) that an MPC of 3/4 produces a multiplier of 4 for the simple reason that
$$[(1 \times £100) + (3/4 \times £100) + (3/4^2 \times £100) + (3/4^3 \times £100) \ldots]$$
is an infinite geometric progression, and infinite geometric progressions we learned, or should have learned, in school add up to definite numbers if the multiplying coefficient is less than 1 in absolute value. In other words $[1 + r + r^2 + r^3 \ldots r^n + \ldots = 1/1 - r,$ if $r < \pm 1.]$ Our MPC, always being less than one, fits the case perfectly. So, when $MPC = 3/4$, $MPS = 1/4$, and the multiplier value is always the inverse of $1 - MPC = MPS$. Put simply, the simple multiplier is always the reciprocal of the marginal propensity to save, which is one of the fundamental 'laws' of Keynesian economic algebra.

Now, any change in investment will produce a multiplied effect on output equal to $1/MPS$, which in our case is 4. Looking back to Figure 2.3, and noting that the addition of I and G to C does not change the slope of the successive $C + I + G$ curves, it follows that the 'marginal propensity to spend' is like MPC equal to 3/4; hence an increase in investment (or C or G) of 25 would raise income by 100. We could demonstrate this by shifting the I curve and hence the $C + 1 + G$ curve up by 25 and reading off the resulting equilibrium level of income along the horizontal axis. But that would clutter up Figure 2.3; besides, the conclusion that the multiplier is 4 is already incorporated in the figure. Let us go back to the C curve when $I = 0$; then the equilibrium level of output is at A; if we now add $I = 25$, we know that the new equilibrium level of output must rise by 100, because only if it does so will $C = 75$ plus $I = 25$ add up to $Y_e = 100$. It must add up to 100 because, by virtue of the 45-degree line, a horizontal distance of 100 must add up to a vertical distance of 100. The multiplier applied to investment is 4, and since investment and government expenditure in our simplified model is purely 'autonomous' and independent of income, the 'marginal propensity to spend' is also 4; that is simply to say that any kind of extra spending will have a quadrupled effect on output or income.

All this, simple as it may be, is a lot to take in at first sight. Experience suggests that it can only be absorbed by doing a few exercises employing actual numbers. Take graph paper, draw a linear consumption function with different $MPCs$, remembering that MPC is nothing more than the slope of C and that a slope of, say, 2/3 is represented by a vertical triangle with two squares down and three square across. Choose a break-even level of income for the consumption function, and then add a given amount for 'autonomous investment'; then solve for the equilibrium level of income and mark off the solution along the horizontal axis. At this point, we get fancy by adding 'induced' to 'autonomous' investment which is expressed by an investment function that is steeper than the consumption function, since more income 'induces' more investment. In consequence, the marginal propensity to spend is greater than MPC and, hence, the multiplier applied to total spending is greater than the multiplier applied solely to consumption. A half-hour spent exploring these and other possibilities with specific numbers will teach you more about the Keynesian theory of income determination than a whole shelf of books about Keynes.

The stark, dramatic Keynesian story told so far needs some qualification. We have in fact been speaking of the 'instantaneous multiplier', paying no attention to the length of time required for successive rounds of spending to affect output. The instantaneous multiplier in an economy may be 4, yet it could take six, twelve or twenty-four months for an extra pount of spending to produce its final quadrupled effect on output. Moreover, we have tacitly assumed that all the multiplied effect operates on real ouput and that none of it raises prices. This may well be true in an economy with considerable excess capacity and unemployed workers, but as the economy approaches and finally reaches its level of maximum potential output, it is not possible to increase output at the going level of prices, at which point higher spending simply ends up in higher prices. In short, the multiplier still operates even in a fully employed economy, but the easy identification of income with output ceases to hold. Indeed, the entire Keynesian multiplier model of income determination may lose most of its explanatory power in an economy operating at or near to its full employment level of output.

The really novel feature of Keynesian economics, brilliantly depicted in the simple 45-degree line version of Keynesian theory, is the underlying thesis that the change in output itself acts as a force equilibrating saving and investment. In all previous theorising about aggregate income, output and employment, it was always the rate of interest that was in the foreground of the forces making for a stable equilibrium. The striking characteristic of Keynesian economics is the extent to which many if not most of Keynes's fundamental conclusions can be set out without even mentioning the rate of interest; the only place where it occurred in our account so far was in relation to investment, and even here, the role of the rate of interest in encouraging or discouraging investment can be ignored without distorting Keynes's basic argument.

All this is not to say that Keynes himself ignored the rate of interest; far from it. In his own day, his iconoclastic 'liquidity preference theory' of interest generated more controversy among economists than his ideas about the consumption function or the multiplier. That theory was iconoclastic because it was a purely monetary theory of interest; that is, it accounted for the rate of interest without reference to the real factors of productivity and thrift that had been the hallmark of all theories of interest since the eighteenth century. Without delving any deeper into this liquidity preference theory of interest, with its catalogue of motives for holding money, it is worth noting that Keynes simply *had* to adopt a monetary theory of interest once he had defined saving to be solely, and investment partly, a function of income, there was simply nothing left to determine the rate of interest except the demand and supply of money. Since Keynes assumed that the money supply was autonomous, which in economic parlance always means 'not explained by economic theory', it followed that the rate of interest depended largely on the demand for money. No wonder that Keynes devoted much of his analytical powers to developing a rich and complex theory of the demand for money-to-hold!

This rather peculiar two-part appearance of Keynesian economics – one in which saving and investment are equilibrated and the other in which the demand and supply of money are equilibrated, with the level of income and the rate of interest serving as tenuous bridges between the two parts – accounts for the instant popularity of John Hicks's *IS* − *LM* interpretation of *The General Theory*. In an article which appeared in 1936 within a few months of the publication of the book, Hicks interpreted *The General Theory* as a theory about an economy with two markets: a market for consumer and investment goods in which the *I = S* equality determined an equilibrium level of output and incidentally an equilibrium level of interest, and a money market in which the *L = M* equality (*L* standing for liquidity preference and *M* for the supply of money) determined an equilibrium level of the interest rate and incidentally an equilibrium level of output. Hicks succeeded in combining both of these equilibrium relationships in one diagram, and in this way produced the standard teaching model of Keynesian economics for intermediate students, just as Samuelson later invented the 45-degree line diagram that immediately became the standard teaching model for beginning students.

Although the Hicksian *IS* − *LM* version of *The General Theory* is one step up from the 45-degree line version, it still falls short of rendering the whole of Keynes's reasoning in the book because, for one thing, it manages to expound Keynesian economics without mentioning the labour market. But one of the striking features of the book that confounded contemporaries was Keynes's surprising conclusion that unemployment is not curable by cutting wages; that, in any case, wages simply cannot be cut; and that, even if they could, this would do more harm than good.

Let us see briefly how the argument goes, because the idea that unemployment is due to 'wages being too high' was influential before

Keynes and has been influential since; in short, we are still wondering whether Keynes was right about the relationship between wages and employment.

Keynes expounded his theory of effective demand in *The General Theory* on the assumption that money wages are constant. It was only in Chapter 19, entitled 'Changes in Money Wages', that he took up the link between wages and employment. Keynes accepted the pre-Keynesian classical assumption that employment depends fundamentally on *real* wages – that is, money wages divided by some index of the level of prices. In other words, to increase employment it was necessary somehow to reduce real wages. Classical reasoning suggested that this could be achieved by getting workers to accept lower money wages and, provided this did not lead to an equivalent fall in prices, this would result in lower real wages. Keynes's first counter-argument was that workers, and particular those in unions, normally resist money wage cuts but are prepared to accept cuts in real wages brought about by rising prices. They do so because money wage cuts disturb the relative wage differences between different groups en shrined in custom and tradition, whereas price increase cause equal misery all round. But workers do not control prices, so there is in fact no way that labour as a whole can reduce real wages.

Nevertheless, despite the resistance of workers to wage cuts, Keynes agreed that money wages would slowly decline in the face of unemployment (after all, they had done so after 1929, although less so in Britain than in the USA). The decline of money wages was capable of stimulating employment in three ways, none of which, he argued, would be likely to be very effective. The first was via the distribution of income. Across-the-board money wage cuts, if passed on to consumers in terms of lower prices, may result in an increase in aggregate real spending power. However, they are likely to be associated with higher profits, with a redistribution of real income from workers to entrepreneurs. Profit receivers typically have a lower propensity to consume than workers, and for that reasons the cut in money wages may actually cause aggregate demand to fall. This effect may be offset by higher investment, but that depends on whether the new level of wages is seen as permanent; if further wage cuts are contemplated, investment may be delayed. In short, there is no guarantee that the redistribution of income from wages to profits will stimulate an increased demand for labour.

The second way in which wage cuts might work is via international competitiveness. *The General Theory* is argued in terms of a closed economy, but Keynes does not deny the obvious contention that a cut in money wages relative to other countries is likely to stimulate employment by ecouraging exports and discouraging imports. Nevertheless, that advantage is bound to be temporary, lasting only as long as other countries do not retaliate by cutting their own wages. On balance, therefore, this is not a sound way of curing unemployment.

The third way in which wage cuts might promote employment is via their effect on the rate of interest. A fall in money wages leading to a fall in prices reduces the demand to hold money for 'transactions motives': whatever money is held by people can conduct more transactions when every transaction costs less; if the supply of money remains unchanged, this causes the rate of interest to fall, depending as it does on the demand for and supply of money. The fall in the rate of interest will stimulate investment, and hence output and employment will rise.

This effect has been labelled the 'Keynes Effect', because it was Keynes's major concession about the ways in which money wage cuts might be expected to affect the demand for labour. Nevertheless, Keynes was sceptical about the *strength* of this effect. Again, he argued, it all depended on the expected future course of wages and prices: the increased uncertainty engendered by wage cuts and their attendant political difficulties and the fear of impending insolvency as falling prices increased the real burden of debt might destroy the confidence of investors and so increase their demand for money for 'precautionary motives'. Hence the rate of interest might actually rise rather than fall.

Besides, if the Keynes Effect was strong enough to restore full employment, it implied that monetary policy working alone could effectively cure unemployment; in other words, wage cuts were not needed. This was Keynes's trump-card-argument. If wage cuts with an unchanged money supply could produce a sufficient fall in the interest rate to stimulate full employment, then a policy of increasing the quantity of money at unchanged money wages would likewise be capable of generating full employment but much less painfully in terms of political unrest.

So we have several reasons for doubting the usefulness of wage cuts as a device for restoring full employment, and moreover, several economic and political reasons for preferring active demand management over a regime in which money wages are flexible. It has been argued that Keynes ignored one other way in which a wage cut might work to restore full employment, similar to but more comprehensive than the Keynes Effect. It is known as the 'Real Balance Effect', according to which a fall in wages and prices increases the real value of net personal wealth; to get rid of the real wealth they do not wish to hold, individuals spend more, and this effect has no stopping place until wages and prices cease to decline at or near full employment. It is now generally agreed that this consideration is sufficient to undo all of Keynes's theoretical arguments against wage cuts, at least in principle; but in practice it is also agreed that such a severe policy of deflation is likely to have such adverse effects on business confidence as to swamp the Real Balance Effect.

There is a real sense in which Chapter 19 is the climax of *The General Theory*, fulfilling a promise Keynes made early in the book that he would fully elucidate the falseness of 'the classical view' that wage cuts are a remedy to unemployment. But notice how inconclusive that chapter really is, depending, as it does, on a whole series of casually made empirical judgements, as well as on a number of equally casual political assessments. Both of these may well have been perfectly correct for the circumstances of the Great Depression, but not necessarily so for different circumstances.

It would be false, therefore, to assert, as is so often asserted in textbooks, that Keynes proved once and for all that cutting money wages will never stimulate employment. However, it would be equally false to argue that Keynesian economics depends on the assumption of rigid money wages, another assertion frequently encountered in the literature. For one thing, if that were true, there would be nothing new in Keynesian economics; the fact that rigid wages can generate unemployment was a commonplace of pre-Keynesian economics. For another, the whole of Chapter 19 is devoted to analysing the effects of flexible money wages, concluding in the policy *recommendation* that they should be kept relatively stable. A recommendation is, surely, not the same thing as an assumption?

3 The Keynesian Revolution

The impact Keynes had on economics with his book *The General Theory* is what is known as the Keynesian Revolution in economic thought. This Keynesian Revolution is one of the most remarkable episodes in the entire history of economic thought; never before had the economics profession been won over so rapidly and so massively to a new economic theory, and nor has it since. Within the space of about a decade, 1936–46, the vast majority of economists throughout the Western world were converted to the Keynesian way of thinking. Many of those early converts felt themselves impelled to repudiate virtually the entire corpus of received economic doctrine, taking up the Keynesian system with an ardour that is more commonly associated with religious conversions. Moreover, it was the younger generation who proved most susceptible to the Keynesian infection; criticism of Keynes came almost solely from the older members of the profession. In short, the Keynesian Revolution comes close to conforming to a 'scientific revolution' as defined by Thomas Kuhn, involving a sense of theoretical 'crisis', the emergence of a radical new 'paradigm', and a pronounced generation gap in the response of scientists to the clash of the old and new paradigms.

Can we explain this phenomenon? That is the question we shall be asking in the pages that follow. The most popular explanation of Keynes's success was that he provided a more ingenious explanation of mass unemployment than did his orthodox contemporaries. I choose my words carefully. It is frequently said that pre-Keynesian or so-called 'classical economics' could not explain the unemployment of the 1930s. But this is careless language, because there was never any problem about 'explaining' unemployment with the aid of pre-Keynesian theory, drawing on the general notion of market imperfections. In particular, unemployment could be and was explained in orthodox terms by real wages being held above market-clearing levels, by protective tariffs, by an overvalued currency (at least in the case of British unemployment before 1931), by rigid prices due to monopolies and cartels, by misguided monetary policies, etc., etc.

It is true that both money and real wages had fallen sharply in the United States from 1929 down to the trough of the Depression in 1933, while all the time American unemployment had worsened rather than improved. The British case was more ambiguous – relative constancy of money wages and gently rising real wages – but nevertheless it was the world-wide persistence of unemployment in the 1930s that gradually sapped confidence in the orthodox explanations. Thus, it is possible to argue that Keynesian economics gave a more convincing explanation of *protracted* mass unemployment than did orthodox theory, and that is why it won over a large part of the professional academic community.

Nevertheless, this still fails to account convincingly for the unprecedented speed with which Keynes conquered economic opinion. The staggering fact remains that Keynesian economics took only twelve years (and by some criteria, only five or six years) to win the approval of the vast majority of professional economists. It is always arbitrary to date the completion of an intellectual revolution, but one obvious and simple measure is the number of years it takes for the new approach to be incorporated into elementary textbooks. The first textbook of elementary economics to expound the Keynesian system was *The Elements of Economics* (1947) by Lorie Tarshis. It failed to catch on, possibly because it stuck too closely to Keynes's own exposition in *The General Theory*. The same year saw the publication of *The Keynesian Revolution* by Lawrence Klein and *The New Economics: Keynes' Influence on Theory and Policy*, an influential collection of papers about Keynesian economics edited by Seymour Harris. But it was the appearance of Paul Samuelson's *Economics: An Introductory Analysis* (1948), twelve years after the publication of *The General Theory*, that marked the final triumph of Keynesianism. The book opened with a section on the determination of national income along entirely Keynesian lines, using the 45-degree line diagram that Samuelson had himself invented in 1939. Samuelson's book soon proved to be the most successful economics textbook of all time, and its popularity brought Keynes to literally millions of students in the USA and elsewhere. It took many more years for Keynes to conquer professional opinion in Germany, Italy and France, but in the USA and Britain the battle was, for all practical purposes, won by 1948.

It could be argued that the apotheosis of Keynes came even earlier in 1944, when the UK White Paper on *Employment Policy*, William Beveridge's *Full Employment in a Free Society*, and *The Economics of Full Employment: Six Studies in Applied Economics* by the Oxford

Institute of Statistics, followed one another within the space of nine months. One could even claim that the battle was won still earlier in 1941 or 1942. A British Budget of 1941 was couched in the spirit and even the letter of Keynes, and we now know that Roosevelt's economic advisors in the White House were committed to the Keynesian framework by 1942. At any rate, what opposition there was to Keynes among academic economists, civil servants and government advisors virtually disappeared during the Second World War, which proved indeed to be something like a laboratory experiment in the effectiveness of Keynesian ideas of demand management. It is the amazing rapidity of the Keynesian ascendancy that poses the problem for any convincing account of the Keynesian Revolution.

At one time, in the early bloom of the Keynesian Revolution, it was common to attribute Keynes's triumph simply to his superior policy proposals. Orthodox economists offered no remedies for the depression except a balanced budget and an all-round deflation to force down real wages; only Keynes advocated a deliberately unbalanced budget and compensatory spending on public works. More recent historical research has thoroughly undermined this mythical picture of Keynes as a 'voice crying in the wilderness'. Much of the mythology that still surrounds popular accounts of the Keynesian Revolution relies on disguising the radical difference in the state of pre-Keynesian economics in the USA and Britain. There were some outstanding economists in the USA who favoured monetary over fiscal measures in dealing with the Depression, but the majority of US economists strongly supported a public works programme financed by borrowing, and went out of their way to attack the concept of an annually balanced government budget as an old-fashioned dogma. Indeed, the erosion of the shibboleth of balanced budgets and the adoption of the doctrine of 'spending America out of depression' had been virtually completed in Washington circles by 1936 without the benefit of Keynes's *General Theory*. Moreover, the US experience with wage deflation discouraged any belief in the efficacy of wage-cutting as a cure for unemployment, even among the conservative critics of the New Deal. In short, US economists inside and outside the universities generally favoured policies before as well as after 1936 which we now think of as Keynesian – and the same is true of Germany and the Scandinavian countries.

Almost as much might be said of Britain, except that the depressed conditions of the 1920s, in contrast to the great American boom of that decade, and the return to the gold standard at the pre-war parity between 1925 and 1931, produced somewhat greater diversity of policy recommendations among British than among US economists. Besides, the case for wage-cutting as a cure for unemployment was always better for Britain than for the United States, first because real wages had declined much less in the 1930s in Britain than in the USA, and second because Britain was more of an open economy than the USA. In addition, the gap between official thinking in Whitehall and the academic community of economists was much greater in Britain than in America. The 'Treasury View' that public spending must crowd out private investment, and thus leave aggregate demand no greater than before, had no standing among British academic economists, but was held by Treasury officials throughout the 1930s. In consequence, Britain alone among the major Western industrial nations eschewed any hint of public works and deficit finance to promote domestic recovery in the 1930s, and instead relied on cheap money, high tariffs, devaluation and a number of supply-side policies. There has long been wide support among British economists for loan-financed public works, but the overvalued pound in the late 1920s produced a small school of 'structuralists', such as Arthur Pigou, Edwin Cannan and Henry Clay, who attributed unemployment to real wages being too high, especially in the declining staple industries. These structuralist arguments largely faded away after Britain left the gold standard in 1931, only to be replaced by the US monetary over-investment theories of the business cycle advocated by Friedrich Hayek, the leader of the Austrian School of Economics, and Lionel Robbins.

According to the Austrian theory of the business cycle, slumps are the necessary consequence of the 'forced saving' associated with undue credit expansion in the previous boom; they should be allowed to run their course like a fever, so as to give way to the healthy boom that will inevitably follow. The protracted nature of the inter-war slump in Britain was explained by the collapse of the gold standard and the proliferation of wage- and price-fixing arrangements that had undermined the natural recuperative powers of the economy. This view, perfectly represented by Lionel Robbins' *The Great Depression* (1934), concluded that wage-cutting, however desirable, was inexpedient, and besides it was the inflexibility of all prices and not just wages that exacerbated the Depression. Little followed from all this in the way of practical action, but the conditions for recovery, Robbins seemed to suggest, were a return to free trade, a stable currency based on the gold standard, and institutional reform attacking the myriad ways in which governments promoted monopolies and cartels. The Hayek-Robbins viewpoint fell on deaf ears and attracted so little attention that Keynes did not even bother in *The General Theory* to mention either Hayek's *Prices and Production* (1931) or Robbins's *Great Depression* (although there was a footnote referring to Robbins), choosing instead to direct all his ammunition against Pigou's highly abstract and profoundly obscure *Theory of Unemployment* (1933). Of course, there was no single canonical text that characterised the whole of British economic thinking on anti-Depression policies, and hence Keynes was virtually driven to invent a straw man of what he called 'classical economics' to dramatise his battle with orthodoxy. Summing up, it is fair to say that there was a pre-Keynesian orthodoxy on policy matters in Britain – free trade, the gold standard, balanced budgets, debt redemption, and structural reforms – but it was a creed of bankers, businessmen, civil servants and politicians, not of academic economists. The economists were largely in agreement on everything except free trade, and in any case were at pains to sink their differences in favour of proposals like easy money and loan-financed public works.

The very first sentence of the preface to *The General Theory* announces that it is a book addressed to Keynes's fellow economists, and therefore that 'its main purpose is to deal with difficult questions of theory and only in the second place with the applications of this theory to practice'. Thus, Keynes attacked 'classical' economists not because they disagreed with him about action to remedy the slump but because he thought that they were wedded to ideas that were inconsistent with the policies they were advocating. Hence the footnote reference to Robbins in *The General Theory*: 'It is the distinction of Professor Robbins that he, almost alone, continues to maintain a distinct scheme of thought, his practical recommendation belonging to the same system as his theory.' What Keynes sought was capitulation on the theoretical front and, as he said in a letter to George Bernard Shaw on January 1, 1935: 'I believe myself to be writing a book on economic theory which will largely revolutionise – not I suppose at once but in the course of the next ten years – the way the world thinks about economic problems', a prediction that proved to be perfectly accurate. Let us remind ourselves once again of the principal theoretical features of Keynesian economics:

1. A shift in method from micro- to macroeconomics, from the long period to the short period, from real to monetary analysis, and

from the variation of prices to the variation of quantities as central objects of analysis.

2. Both aggregate consumption and aggregate savings are taken to be stable functions of income, but investment is treated at least partly as autonomous, inherently volatile, and subject to pervasive uncertainty.

3. Saving and investment are said to be carried out by different people for different reasons and are only brought into equilibrium by changes of income itself.

4. The rate of interest is explained in monetary terms as a function of the stock demand for money interacting with an exogenously determined supply of money.

5. Real wages are treated as determined by the volume of employment rather than the other way around.

At the bottom of the entire schemea is the Great Heresy that an equilibrium level of income and output need not correspond to a situation of full employment, and indeed that the economy is very likely to get stuck in a low-level unemployment equilibrium trap, there being no spontaneous, self-adjusting mechanism that will necessarily drive the economy to employ the entire labour force and to utilise the capital stock to full capacity. There is no doubt that it was this heresy combined with Keynes's demonstration of the 'paradox of thrift' – in an economy with unemployment more saving means more, not less, unemployment – that gave Keynesian economics its subversive, left-wing coloration and which earned it so much enmity from conservatives, particularly in the United States. In places in *The General Theory*, Keynes went so far as to suggest that the poor have higher marginal propensities to consume than the rich, implying that ouput and hence employment could be raised by redistribution of income from the rich to the poor. In addition, he suggested that capitalism, when left to its own devices, was doomed to 'secular stagnation', not just in the distant but possibly in the near future. No wonder, then, that *The General Theory* proved irresistible to young economists, radicalised by years of depression. And yet all this does not exhaust the list of appealing features in *The General Theory*.

One of Keynes's critical analytical decisions in moving away from his *Treatise on Money* towards *The General Theory* was to abandon the type of sequence of 'period analysis' that characterised monetary economics and the business cycle literature of the 1920s and instead to adopt the now familiar static equilibrium mode of analysis in which all the relevant variables of the model refer to a single period of time. It was this decision to handle essentially dynamic problems with a static apparatus that led him to define income, saving and investment in such a way as to make realised saving identically equal to realised investment, which related consumption and income via the consumption function, and which in turn defined the instantaneous multiplier as the reciprocal of the marginal propensity to save. The use of this equilibrium method confused many of Keynes's earlier readers, who were accustomed to price theory employing comparative statics and monetary theory employing period analysis, but it was precisely this heterodox use of statis equilibrium analysis applied to a monetary economy that was out of equilibrium that gave Keynes's theory its allegoric rigour and analytical simplicity.

In addition, Keynes worked hard to define all his variables in operational terms, relating them whenever possible to actual or potentially available data. In so doing he rode on the back of the statistical revolution that was already well on the way when *The General Theory* was published. Colin Clarke's *The National Income 1924–1931* (1932) and Simon Kuznets's *National Income 1929–1932* (1934) testify to a tradition of national income accounting that predates the publication of *The General Theory*. Nevertheless, Keynes's treatment of income as the chief determinant of consumption and the importance assigned in his theory to final outlays of consumption and investment, not to mention the one-period definitions of saving and investment, gave an enormous stimulus to the statistical measurement of income and outlays. Official estimates of national income appeared first in the United States in 1935, the year before *The General Theory*. By 1939, official and unofficial estimates were available for thirty-three countries, and it is no accident that the first official estimates in the United Kingdom were prepared in 1940 by James Meade and Richard Stone, two of Keynes's disciples, stimulated by Keynes's own use of national income estimates to analyse the prospective inflationary gap in *How to Pay for the War* (1940). By the end of the Second World War, official national income accounts appeared in almost all industrialised countries and were invariably presented in the $Y = C + I + G$ format of Keynesian economics.

There was a pre-Keynesian macroeconomics, but it was contentious, complex and cast almost entirely in non-operational terms, such as the degree of 'roundaboutness' of the economy, the level of hoarding and dishoarding, forced saving, overindebtedness, under-consumption and the like. Keynes achieved a drastic simplification of macroeconomics or, more cynically expressed, he achieved the optimum level of difficulty for intellectual success – not so simple as to be immediately accessible without some effort and yet not so complex as virtually to defy comprehension. An essential additional ingredient in the success of *The General Theory* was its openendedness and sheer fecundity. Keynes was fond of the method of overkill or arriving at the same conclusion from several different angles. Thus, Chapter 17 of *The General Theory* on 'The Essential Properties of Interest and Money' seeks to produce the central Keynesian conclusion that 'unemployment equilibrium' is possible and even likely without the aid of the building blocks developed in the previous sixteen chapters. Likewise, as we saw before, Chapter 19 on the 'Changes in Money Wages' resorts to as many as half a dozen different arguments intended to demonstrate the impracticability and undesirability of cutting money wages as a cure for unemployment. *The General Theory* is littered with digressions, puzzles requiring solution, and a wealth of theoretical hints awaiting further development. This efflorescence of ideas, a sense of the cup running over, was one of the elements of its appeal. It is a poorly constructed book that frequently reads more like a set of random notes than a systematic treatise, but even this quality of undue haste only enhanced its intellectual effectiveness.

Have we now finally accounted for the Keynesian Revolution? Not in my opinion. Economists do not adopt new theories just because they are simple, elegant, rigorous, ideologically convenient and politically appealing. They demand that their implications should be confirmed by the available data. In the final analysis, what they really find persuasive is that the theory should predict some novel, hitherto unsuspected facts, which now suddenly make sense by being 'fitted into' a more general framework. Keynesian economics in fact came equipped with a number of new predictions.

The principal novel prediction of Keynesian economics is that the value of the instantaneous multiplier is greater than unity, and that the more than proportional impact of an increase in investment on income applies just as much to public as to private investment, and indeed just as much to consumption as to investment spending. In other words, fiscal policy is capable, at least in principle, of raising real income up to the full employment ceiling within a single time period.

The notion that a government can spend its way out of depression predated Keynes's *General Theory* and derived from the quantity of theory of money, at least in its short version. David Hume, one of the founders of the quantity theory of money, had argued as early as the eighteenth century in favour of creeping inflation: a steady continual increase in the supply of money is partly transmitted to real output and is therefore not simply inflationary. The monetary writing of a number of early twentieth-century economists, including the young Keynes himself, had long familiarised economists with the short-run, disequilibrium interpretation of the quantity theory of money; in fact, this was the standard pre-Keynesian framework for demonstrating the efficacy of a loan-financed public works programme. The trouble was that the argument was loose and imprecise and hence was vulnerable to objections based either on the'Treasury View'or on the sheer administrative costs of mounting such schemes at short notice.

Keynes learned from Richard Kahn, his young pupil, how to calculate, however crudely, a precise value for the income multiplier, and in so doing he placed the case for demand management on an entirely new footing by making it seem incontrovertible. The case relied on the notion of consumption as a stable function of income and *The General Theory's* definition of saving and investment as two sides of the same coin, and it followed as a matter of logic that any increase in real income and employment could be achieved by a sufficiently large autonomous increase in consumption, or investment or government expenditure. This was a novel prediction, not only in the sense that it was unknown before Keynes's *General Theory*, but also because it was an unsuspected implication of the conept of the consumption function combined with the peculiar Keynesian defini-tions of savings and investment; it was not just any consumption function but one in which the marginal propensity to consume lies between zero and one, is smaller than the average propensity to consume (the ratio of consumption to income), and declines as income rises.[1] These three characteristics of the Keynesian consump-tion function were simply asserted by Keynes in *The General Theory*, but all three mini-predictions were in fact confirmed in 1942 by the first set of comprehensive national income data for the United States.

The same thing is *not* true of the greater-than-unity value of the expenditure multiplier, Keynes's principal prediction. Keynes him-self estimated the British multiplier to be 1.5, but some of his

---

1. In other words, Keynes did not believe that the consumption function is a straight line as depicted in Figure 2.3. He thought that it was bow-shaped, so that people would consume a smaller and smaller proportion of additional income as income rose.

disciples produced estimates in 1938, 1939 and 1941 of between 2.0 and 3.0, and in one case of even more than 3.0. Because of various 'leakages' into taxes, imports and savings, as well as the slow rate at which the secondary and tertiary effects show up, the true figure in most countries, we now think, is perhaps only just in excess of 1.0. In consequence, some revisionist economic historians have recently expressed doubts about Keynes's remedies in the circumstances of the 1930s, arguing that the fiscal stimulus designed to produce full employment in the severely depressed pre-war British economy would have had to have been so large as to entail physical planning on a war-time scale.

It is worth noting that Keynes himself would *not* have been as startled by the recent revisionist interpretations of the inter-war British economy as we are. He was perfectly aware that government budgets in the 1930s were so small that any budgetary deficit could only have had a miniscule effect on national income. For example, the fall in income experienced by the United States and the United Kingdom between 1929 and 1933 was so great that public expenditure would have had to have increased by 50–70 per cent to have filled in the gap. However, that is only to say that Keynes, at least in *The General Theory*, did not actually advocate budgetary deficits as a tool of stabilisation policy,[2] but rather monetary policy in conjunction with the stabilisation of investment by means of a permanent rise in the proportion of income spent by governments – that is what was meant by his famous recommendation of 'the socialisation of investment' in the closing pages of his book.

Let us sum up. It may be convincingly argued that the Keynesian system was never put to the test before the war, that budgetary deficits in the 1930s were never large enough to produce the Keynesian results – in short, that Hitler's rearmament programme was the only New Deal that actually succeeded in eliminating unemployment, but that in no way affects the point I have been trying to make: *The General Theory* gained adherents because Keynes made a novel prediction that seemed highly likely to be true. The

---

2. Keynes refers only twice in the book to budgetary deficits: once incidentally to built-in stabilisers – the automatic tendency for government spending to go up and taxes to go down as income falls – and once to suggest ironically that publicly financed pyramid-building, gold-mining, and burying old bottles filled with bank notes, while not as 'sensible' as a housing programmes, would be better than nothing as a way of dealing with unemployment.

virtual disappearance of unemployment during the Second World War was perceived to be, rightly or wrongly, a dramatic corroboration of the central Keynesian prediction. In the same way, the full employment and overall employment conditions of the 1950s and 1960s were everywhere attributed to the deliberate pursuit by governments of Keynesian policies, although it was in fact private investment that filled the post-war gap in effctive demand. In other words, the evidence for Keynes's central prediction is not compelling even now, but that is simply to say that what seems compelling at one time in history is not necessarily seen to be persuasive with the benefit of hindsight forty or fifty years later.

The principal new prediction of the Keynesian system was that fiscal policy by itself is capable of generating a full-employment level of income. But there were many other novel facts predicted by *The General Theory*, some of which were influential in attracting additional adherents to Keynesianism: for example, that there are significant differences in the marginal propensities to consume of households at different income levels; that the interest-elasticity of investment is very low; that, on the contrary, the interest-elasticity of the demand for money is very high; and, finally, that the average propensity to consume of the community tends to decline as national income rises, indicating that the threat of secular stagnation in mature economies will get worse as they grow richer. It turned out eventually that aggregate consumption and saving is relatively insensitive to change in the distribution of income, but in the 1930s young American Keynesians placed as much emphasis on income redistribution as on deficit spending as a way out of the Depression. Similarly, Keynes himself never ceased to believe that investment was sufficiently responsive to reductions in the rate of interest to make monetary policy a potent instrument for raising employment additional to fiscal policy. But a number of empirical studies by young British Keynesians soon showed that the interest-elasticity of investment was not much greater than zero, and this encouraged the belief that Keynesianism was tantamount to the thesis that private investment is bound to fall short of full employment. Lastly, imminent stagnation was a constant theme in the Keynesian literature, and, in the influential writings of Alvin Hansen, Keynes's leading American disciple, was converted into the very essence of the Keynesian message. To show how widely stagnationism was held, it is only necessary to mention that it was primarily responsible for the almost universal belief among economists in 1945 that the post-war era would commence with a sharp slump. The doctrine that industrialised countries in the twentieth century faced a chronic deficiency of effective demand because private investment was bound to fall behind full-employment savings was one of keynes's novel predictions; it was a false prediction and it was not essential to Keynesian economics, but it was nevertheless a prediction that gained him followers in the early days of the Keynesian Revolution.

Another one of Keynes's erroneous predictions was the proposition that the average propensity to save is a declining function of income, a prediction that was at first confirmed by cross-section budget studies of family expenditure patterns, which literally exploded in the late 1930s and early 1940s. In 1946, Kuznets's *National Product Since 1869* brought home the distinction between cross-section data that confirmed, and time-series data that refuted the prediction of a negative association between the saving-income ratio and the level of national income. In other words, when we compare rich and poor households at one moment in time, it is true that richer households save a larger fraction of their income than do poorer households; but when we compare households over time it is not true that they save a large fraction of their income as they become richer. The attempt to reconcile this contradiction resulted in the Duesenberry Relative Income Hypothesis, the Modigliani Life Cycle Hypothesis and the Friedman Permanent Income Hypothesis. These hypotheses spanned more than a decade of theoretical and empirical work on the savings function inspired by Keynes's *General Theory*, but nevertheless travelled light-years away from the rather simplistic consumption and savings function originally stipulated by Keynes.

Keynes had deliberately assumed a closed economy in *The General Theory*, but the spending multiplier applies just as much to the spending of foreigners on exports as it does to domestic spending. That the foreign trade multiplier is typically greater than unity and that income effects are quantitatively more important than price effects in bringing the balance of payments into equilibrium are other new predictions of the Keynesian system, and followers of Keynes soon explored them, even if Keynes himself ignored them. The invention of the Phillips Curve in 1958 and the manner in which it was grafted on to Keynesian economics is yet another example of the amazing fertility of the Keynesian system. Of course, we have now moved well beyond the year 1948 which, we earlier argued, marked the completion of the Keynesian Revolution as a process of gaining the endorsement of the economics profession. But it is worth remembering that there is a sense in which the Keynesian Revolution is still going on. After degenerating in the 1960s and being virtually supplanted by 'monetarism' and 'rational expectations', Keynesian economics has made something of a comeback in recent years. Macroeconomics is once again trying to explain the failure of labour markets to clear in the face of unemployment – that is, to give new theoretical answers to the old Keynesian question. The spectre of Keynes continues to haunt macroeconomics, as is shown by the endless books and articles on 'What Keynes really meant', 'should have meant', and 'must have meant'.

What, in conclusion, accounts for the Keynesian Revolution? What makes economists adopt a new theory? Economics is not like physics; nor it is just a body of substantive findings about the judgements and political preconceptions of economists. Nevertheless, new economic doctrines do not find a ready audience among economists unless they can promise to produce new findings about the economy that are eventually confirmed by historical and statistical analysis. Thus, it was not just ideology, an animus against capitalism, a desire to cock a snook at the older generation, or simply a preference for something new, that drove economists into the Keynesian camp. Keynes had caught a measure of substantive truth about the working of an economic system that had not been vouchsafed to his predecessors, and that is fundamentally why economists in the 1930s adopted Keynesian economics.

4 Talking to Leading Economists about Keynes

Brian Reddaway

Brian Reddaway (1913–) studied economics at Cambridge University in the early 1930s, and Keynes was one of his supervisers. Later he published the very first review of *The General Theory* to appear anywhere in the world. His long and distinguished career included a Professorship at Cambridge (1969–80), membership of the UK National Board of Prices and Incomes (1967–71) and the post that Keynes himself had once held, Editor of *The Economic Journal* (1971–6).

I travelled to Cambridge to talk to Brian Reddaway, who is now living in retirement. His entire life has been spent in Cambridge in contact with Keynes himself and with matters Keynesian.

BLAUG: Professor Reddaway, your first contact with Keynes was as an undergraduate at Cambridge in the early 1930s. Would you like to tell us how you met Keynes?

REDDAWAY: I went to Keynes as part of what we call in Cambridge 'supervisions', which the Oxford people call 'tutorials'. That is a system which is very demanding on staff manpower, but which we at Oxbridge regard as the key to excellence of teaching. The arrangement is that students go in groups of two or three to one of the staff members and before they go they have to write an essay on a problem which has been set by the staff member. They hand in that essay in advance and the staff member reads it through, and if he feels like it he writes remarks in the margin and usually he gives some sort of mark for it.

My main supervisor at Cambridge was Gerald Shove and not Keynes. But I was lucky, as were all the people doing economics in King's, which was my college, because Keynes was a very special sort of Fellow who spent most of his working activities in London but who came to Cambridge for a long weekend every week in term time. We went in groups of two or three to him in just the same way as we went to other supervisors. We wrote our essays and he did his stuff and then we had a discussion of them over a period of about an hour. But in his case he chose subjects which were of special interest to him or on which he had something very special to say. So in that, in a way, we were a very privileged lot of students.

The very first essay that I wrote for him was on the subject of free trade and protection. This was in 1932, and the current conventional wisdom of the economists was that free trade was the best system. I confess I had some slight doubts about whether that was always the case. So I wrote my essay and rather tentatively suggested that free imports without free trade in the other countries was not necessarily the best system. Keynes was, I think, rather interested in this essay. He gave me a nice high mark and he wrote 'Good' at the bottom, but he added that I had not dealt with an aspect that he would discuss at the supervision. This aspect was the difference it made if you had a large amount of unemployment in the country. How you could in a sense get rid of part of that unemployment on to other countries and improve your own position by having a surplus on your balance of payments, induced through protection. And he explained that it would really be better if you stimulated internal investment, rather than doing this, and certainly it would be better from the world point of view. So that was the kind of thing that happened, and very fortunately on that occasion I made some elaborate notes immediately after the supervision of what he had said.

BLAUG: Another one of your contacts with Keynes was the famous Monday Club, was it not?

REDDAWAY: Indeed. This was something where one was not dependent on being in King's College; it was drawing on the whole of the university. And the system was that he invited, on the recommendation of people in other colleges, the best students to be members of this club. And honorary members, so to speak, were the research students and the lecturers and Fellows of other colleges who wanted to come along.

The system was that somebody wrote a paper on an economic subject of their own choice and read it out. After the author had finished the exposition, then there were a series of contributions, starting with the undergraduates. And if more than six undergraduates came, as was normally the case, they drew lots for who would speak first, second, and so on up to six. After the undergraduates came the research students if they wanted to talk, and then the lecturers, and finally Keynes would sum it up in some remarks from the chair.

BLAUG: Now what were your impressions as a student? I mean, Keynes read your essays and marked them. You heard him commenting on speakers on Monday night. You must have been aware that he was well known. Of course, you had no sense of how famous he was eventually to become. What was your impression of him as a teacher?

REDDAWAY: Well, he was not a teacher in the normal sense because he wasn't responsible for the undergraduates, he was a bonus. I think the main impression which one got was that if he thought well of you nothing was too much trouble. He would do a good deal to help, not only in the formal meetings but to some extent outside as well. In my own case, after I had graduated, I wrote an essay for a prize which was open to people who had graduated in the last three years, and Keynes generously said he would send it to Macmillan, who were his publishers, and would recommend that they publish it as a book. Well, that was so to speak after he had been a teacher, but it was symptomatic of his desire to help. He helped me to get my first job as well. But in the pure teaching way he was quite an inspiration if you were on the right lines with him. But he didn't suffer fools gladly. We didn't have many fools in King's undergraduates at that time, but there were one or two who didn't get as helpful comments from him as the rest of us did. And in the Monday Club he could be rather devastating if people advanced silly views in the exposition

BLAUG: Was there a feeling about him among the students that he was somebody special, or was he simply another one of the teachers?

REDDAWAY: Oh, he was somebody special. In the first place he wasn't a regular teacher; he was a sort of supernumerary person doing something different from what the others were doing. Secondly, one had read or at least seen his earlier books – *The Economic Consequences of the Peace, The Treatise on Money*, and so on. One knew of him as very influential. In the course of my study, he produced the newspaper articles on 'The Means to Prosperity', which were very pertinent to the economic situation as it was. He was one of the group of economists who had sent a letter to *The Times* in the midst of the Depression, advocating a spending campaign rather than an economy campaign. There was no dobut that we knew we were dealing with somebody rather special.

BLAUG: When you graduated, you said that Keynes helped you to get your first job and was even responsible for you going to Australia in 1936 to take up a post as a Research Fellow at the University of Melbourne. You went off to Australia and Keynes gave you an advance copy of *The General Theory* to read. Then what?

REDDAWAY: When I arrived in Melbourne, there was a lot of interest in this new book and I read a paper about it to an economics club which used to meet regularly. I was then asked to do a review of this book for the *Economic Record*, which is the equivalent of *The Economic Journal* in the UK. So I buckled to it and I think I delivered the manuscript to the *Economic Record* in May of 1936, and they got things printed then more rapidly than we seem to do now. I appeared in the September 1936 issue of the *Economic Record*.

BLAUG: Yours was in fact the first review of *The General Theory* to appear anywhere in the English-speaking world – indeed, anywhere in the world. It was seven months after the publication of the book. Now, looking back on this review you must have wondered over the years whether some of your first reactions to the book were surprising in view of later developments. How do you feel about this review now?

REDDAWAY: I did in fact go back to that review when I was

preparing the Keynes Lecture for the British Academy in 1983. What struck me then was, firstly, that I had not cottoned on to that fact that the treatment in Keynes's book was of an equilibrium position rather than a process of movement. I quoted in the lecture the bit which said that one could visualise different levels of Gross National Product, as we would now say, and that the Gross National Product would settle down at the level that would give the amount of saving from the community equal to the amount of investment which was being done. Well that is an equilibrium position. Keynes made no real attempt to trace how one would get there. I completely failed to make this point in the review.

But on the other hand, I think I did bring out fairly clearly the inter-connections in static equilibrium of a number of variables, which mutually determine the position of all of them. And, although it is perhaps presumptuous to say it, I did get a letter from Keynes saying that he had read my review and thought I had done a good job, or something of this kind.

I also failed properly to face up to the possibility of changing prices. One of the features of *The General Theory* was that the emphasis changed from the traditional one of analysing what determined the general level of prices, which would then perhaps have an effect on employment and output, to analysing what determined the general level of employment. Well, in my Keynes Lecture of 1983 I did emphasise that one has to think of both of these and not just of one, and that there are other variables as well. So I don't know whether Keynes would have given me a high mark for that review, perhaps he would, but I can understand other people giving slightly lower marks.

BLAUG: Were you struck when you first read *The General Theory* about how little of it actually addresses questions of policy, how theoretical a book it really is?

REDDAWAY: I cannot honestly say whether I was surprised at the time. I agree with what you're saying and I suppose it's particularly ironic that Keynesian economics has come to be popularly associated with the idea of government spending to get out of a depression, whilst there is practically nothing in *The General Theory* about fiscal policy at all. In so far as measures were to be taken, there was to be monetary policy to bring down the rate of interest and to stimulate investment.

But I suppose that as a human being rather than a skilled critic, I felt that Keynes's views on policy matters were part of my general knowledge. There had been this very important set of articles on 'The Means of Prosperity'. There had been this letter to *The Times* with a number of other economists. And in Keynes's teaching of me, the idea of using policies to promote full employment was a commonplace. I suppose I probably ought to have stressed in the review that there was actually very little of this in the book; instead I picked out some of the policy bits that were there as giving the book cogency.

I think I ought to add one very important point in relation to policies. Keynesianism is, as I said, rather freely associated with spending a lot of money to get out of depressions. And that might well be linked with his writing on 'The Means of Prosperity'. But Keynes also used his general approach, his theory as you call it, to deal with the situation in which demand was excessive. The classic example is his pamphlet on *How To Pay For the War*, where the war was creating excess demand through large government expenditure. And the system of ideas evolved in *The General Theory* was used to present a policy for raising the propensity to save, if only more or less involuntarily through the collection of taxes, which would be refunded after the war as deferred credits. Those two, *The Means of Prosperity* and *How To Pay For the War* are very much two sides of one coin. They both involve the use of policy measures by the government to deal with a level of aggregate demand, which was too low in the case of *The Means to Prosperity* and too high in wartime.

* * *

Donald Moggridge

Donald Moggridge (1943–   ) is Professor of Economics at the University of Toronto in Canada, but he spent over ten years at Clare College, Cambridge, editing the *Collected Writings of John Maynard Keynes* in thirty volumes. He is also a recognised authority on British monetary and financial policy of the 1920s. His little book *Keynes* (1975) has no rival for its size as an intellectual biography of Keynes.

Keynes published *The Treatise on Money* in 1930. It was savagely reviewed, and within a year or so Keynes came to share the view of most of his critics: it was a good book but it was also seriously flawed. It took him six more years to work out the content of *The General Theory*. Somehow, in those six years, the Keynesian Revolution was born. But how? I discussed that question with Donald Moggridge,

the editor of Keynes's *Collecting Writings*, while both of us were
sitting in Keynes's former room, in King's College, Cambridge.

BLAUG: What was *The Treatise on Money* trying to do?

MOGGRIDGE: I think one could say that what Keynes was trying to do
in *The Treatise* was to define much more exactly the channels through
which monetary influences worked as a first step to devising a set of
guidelines and rules for policy-making. Now once you do that it
seems that you are reworking the old Marshallian Cambridge cash
balances approach and elaborating the various varieties of bank
deposits and the demand for various kinds of monetary assets, but
also spelling out much more completely, following Robertson, the
savings/investment nexus which of course had not been that clear in
Marshall.

BLAUG: Can you see the seeds of the later *General Theory* in *The
Treatise*?

MOGGRIDGE: There are several bits of analysis that just get carried
over completely, in the sense that you can find 'liquidity preference'
in *The Treatise* without any great difficulty. You can find something
that looks like 'the marginal efficiency of capital'; in fact it is probably
better analysed in *The Treatise* than in *The General Theory*. The
distinction between savers and investors is very strongly dealt with in
The Treatise and again that gets carried over into *The General
Theory*. So, there are various elements that are common to the two
books. Of course, the way they are put together and the types of
analysis are very different.

BLAUG: Why do you think Keynes became dissatisfied with *The
Treatise* almost as soon as he had published it?

MOGGRIDGE: Well, I think that it almost immediately ran into
several fundamental criticisms that came through two routes. In one
case they came from reviewers of the book in the journals. Here one
thinks of Friedrich Hayek, of Dennis Robertson, and in another way,
of course, of Ralph Hawtrey. Secondly, a lot of the criticisms that
were published were echoed by the so-called 'circus', the group of
younger economists around Keynes. One is thinking particularly of
Richard Kahn, Joan Robinson, Piero Sraffa, James Meade and
Austin Robinson. It appears that Keynes took criticisms more
seriously if they were echoed by someone close to him. If Hayek
makes a point, and let's say Kahn or Sraffa re-emphasises it, then
Keynes really takes it on board, whereas if it is something mentioned
by Hayek that isn't echoed internally, he often brushes it aside.

In the course of late 1930 and early 1931 there were adverse comments by close associates on a number of fundamental positions taken up in *The Treatise*. For example, before Keynes had published the book he sent proofs to Hawtrey, and Hawtrey came back with voluminous criticisms which Keynes had not had time to read until after publication. One of the points that Hawtrey made was that output was more or less assumed fixed: *The Treatise* was really a treatise about price movements and not about output movement. Also, Hawtrey pointed out that a lot of the analysis was effectively tautological, that the so-called 'fundamental equations' of *The Treatise* were not motivated in any sort of appropriate way to get the results that Keynes wanted. That gets picked up in another way in Kahn's Multiplier, which again, of course, is echoed by other people. Kahn and Robertson between them suggested that a lot of Keynes's results depended on the peculiarities of definition adopted: if you relaxed those definitions slightly, the results disappeared.

BLAUG: Apart from these technical criticisms about the apparatus of *The Treatise*, why was this criticism of Hawtrey, that the book is really about price movements, taken so seriously? After all, price movements are what monetary economics had always been traditionally about? Was Keynes at this early date already interested in analysing the determination of output?

MOGGRIDGE: I think that he thought that *The Treatise*, although it was written in terms of traditional monetary theory and therefore fundamentally concerned with prices, was more general than that in the sense that a lot of the discussion surrounding the fundamental equations did concern movements in output. For someone like Hawtrey to say that the supporting discussion couldn't be borne by the formal analysis was really rather devastating, irrespective of what was going on in the real world.

BLAUG: Now the interesting thing is the way Keynes reacted to these criticisms. I mean, so many economists, great men in general, when attacked after having written a great treatise, try to defend it, try to repair it, try to amend it. Instead, Keynes simply ditched it and started all over again on another great book that was to become *The General Theory*. That is very odd. It suggests that right at the back of his mind there was an objective which *The Treatise* failed to achieve and which he hoped perhaps to achieve with a new book. Or is there some other explanation for the strange way Keynes reacted to criticisms of *The Treatise*?

MOGGRIDGE: Well, I think there are, let's say, about three bits in answer to that. The first is that if you look at Keynes over his entire career, he lost a large number of important arguments and yet it never seemed to bother him. That may explain why he was so influential, in the sense that he could change his mind, although it might be hard to shift him. The second is that, at least initially, he didn't think he was junking *The Treatise*; if you look at the preface to the Japanese edition of *The Treatise*, which was written at the end of 1931, it sounds as if the new book was going to be a repair job. Actually, if you look at early drafts of *The General Theory* they are all cast in terms of *The Treatise*, in the sense that he is working out of *The Treatise*, effectively trying to repair the damage. It is only much later on, getting into 1933 to 1934, that we get a new presentation resembling what we now know as *The General Theory*. Thirdly, is it true that Keynes had some underlying goal that he wanted to achieve? I am less certain. I don't think that there was some deep-seated need, let's say, to provide a justification for public works: well, you try one in 1924, you try another between 1929 and 1931, and then you try another in *The General Theory*. If only because the justification for public works, of course, in *The Treatise*, is a special case that takes up less than half a page of two volumes. I think one might argue, especially if one reads the surrounding correspondence, that he wasn't perfectly happy with *The Treatise* even before it was published. Just before publication, he told his mother that he had been at it too long and it actually probably didn't really hang together, at least aesthetically it didn't. Nevertheless, I suspect that if the world had said that here was the greatest book that has ever been published in economics, Keynes probably would never have written *The General Theory*. The fact is that the book was mauled both in published reviews and in formal discussion with those whom Keynes was coming to trust most.

*　*　*

Robert Skidelsky

Robert Skidelsky (1939–   ) is Professor of International Rela-
tions at the University of Warwick. After an early book on the
attitude of the British Labour Party to the slump of the 1930s,
he wrote a biography of Mosley, an early follower of Keynes's
views on public works and later the notorious leader of the
British fascist party. Finally, he turned to his biography of
Keynes, the first volume of which appeared in 1987 to much
acclaim, to be followed by two more volumes in the early 1990s.

It was natural to turn from the modern editor of Keynes's writings to
the modern biographer of Keynes, Robert Skidelsky, who now lives
at Tilton, Keynes's former country home in Sussex, where I inter-
viewed him. I began with questions about Keynes's personality
before turning to more substantial matters.

BLAUG: Professor Skidelsky, Keynes was a man of many facets: he was an economist, he moved among artists and philosophers, and he led a somewhat colourful private life. Do you think that these many sides of his personality and his life were in any way connected?

SKIDELSKY: That's an interesting question. It's one that has often been posed and it's bound to be posed, because Keynes was not only a great economist, but he was also a member of a very powerful literary and artistic group, the Bloomsbury Group, which led the attack on Victorian values. And so people naturally wondered what the connection is between Keynes as a member of this cultural group and Keynes as the founder of Keynesian economics. Keynes was, for example, a great friend of Lytton Strachey, whose *Eminent Victorians* subtly undermined the whole belief system of the previous generation. Keynes was very influenced by Lytton Strachey, particularly in the way he wrote. Keynes adopted Strachey's ironic style of writing about Victorian economic virtues. And that's very clear in *The Economic Consequences of the Peace* itself when he discussed Victorian attitudes to saving. He talks about saving as the great duty of the Victorians, the great religion of the Victorian age. And then when he talks about the people's attitudes to the gold standard, you have exactly the same tone. He discussed their attachment to the gold standard almost in Freudian terms.

In all of that you see the influence of his cultural milieu, the modernism of his time, as he would have picked it up from his membership of the Bloomsbury Group. Now I am not saying that all Keynes's economic positions can't be justified in terms of economic analysis and also by reference to the unemployment problem of the time. But the roots of those positions lie deep in his own personality and lie deep in the values of his friends.

BLAUG: What about some of Keynes's political attitudes? For example, the late Sir Roy Harrod, the official biographer of Keynes, often spoke of Keynes as being influenced by what he called 'the presuppositions of Harvey Road'. Now what exactly was meant by those presuppositions?

SKIDELSKY: Well, this links up with what I have just said. Although Keynes was in revolt against Victorian values, he was a Victorian as well. He was born in 1883 in the Victorian age. His parents were great Victorians, characteristically representative Victorians of that period. And I suppose one of the things Roy Harrod meant was that Keynes had a very strong inherited sense of duty that was bred into him by his parents. He couldn't fiddle while Rome burned. He couldn't opt out of the problems of a collapsing society. So, although his values tended to be personal and private, he played a full part in the public life of his day and he was driven to do so. That's one very, very strong presupposition of Harvey Road.

Another presupposition of Harvey Road is that England would continue to be governed by a civilised, responsible and educated élite. Keynes didn't believe that democracy would ever have a very disturbing effect on the government of the country. He had a view of politics and the political process that is now very old-fashioned. He didn't see that political process as a vote-buying system in a competitive market, as modern analysts of politics have tended to do. He believed in a disinterested ruling class, and therefore he believed that that class could be entrusted with quite a lot of power which wouldn't be abused. That is the second point.

But I have got one more point to add to that, and that is he had, like many Victorians and early twentieth-century people of his kind, a quite exaggerated faith in the ability of social science to solve problems. Very characteristic of the early twentieth century. We have lost a lot of it now. In a famous remark to the Macmillan Committee, he said we were approaching the time when the science of monetary policy would be as uncontentious as the science of electricity. That was something that couldn't be said today.

BLAUG: Isn't it striking how similar those presuppositions were to the beliefs of the Fabians? I mean, Sidney and Beatrice Webb would also have been the first to have said that England is basically governed by an intellectual élite, that if only the people with the right ideas are in government, everything will be run correctly, and that social science is sufficiently developed to solve the outstanding social and economic problems. Here we have people on different sides of the political fence really agreeing about certain political presuppositions.

SKIDELSKY: Absolutely – the mind-set of the first half of the twentieth century. Keynes wasn't only a great man, but he was also a man of his time, and certain presuppositions of that kind, which are really a reaction to the decline of religion, I think, and the need to find alternative sources of authority, led people to believe in those kind of things – the fear of democracy and the need to control democracy. If you could control democracy and guide it by an intellectual elite equipped with social science, you would really have found some way of overcoming the problem of social disorder and social chaos, which the loss of religious belief had opened up. I think that was the mind-set of the time.

BLAUG: Do you think Keynes was a welfarist, or have his views on the welfare state been misrepresented?

SKIDELSKY: Yet, what does one mean by welfarist here? I think if one asks: did he believe that when governments spent a lot of money, as he thought they should, it should be spent mainly on creating and sustaining a welfare state? I think his answer would have been no. In that sense, I don't think he was welfarist. You remember the phrase 'the socialisation of investment', which he uses in *The General Theory*? He meant that investment should be the focus of public spending. He wasn't interested very much in other kinds of public spending, he didn't write much about them at all; it was investment that was the problem, and investment was the key to the solution. That was the beginning and end of *The General Theory* really.

Now, if one takes the question a bit further, because I think that's what's implied in it, which is what was Keynes's attitude in general to the Left and to social reform, I think it is very interesting. He always called himself a man of the Left, thought of himself as a man of the Left, but at the same time completely repudiated socialism. Repeatedly, continuously, he said that he had no time for socialism, either as an economic doctrine or – this is less clear – as an end. If you take it as an economic doctrine, he had no time for public ownership. He never believed in public ownership as a means of controlling the economy, as a means of controlling the level of investment, or indeed as something that was more efficient than private enterprise in producing wealth. He believed that you had to have the profit motive and you had to have private enterprise if you wanted to solve the problem of poverty. I think that's all explicit, and that's one big divide from socialists. This doesn't mean to say he didn't work through the Labour Party. He tried to get his ideas increasingly through to the Labour Party but he wasn't socialist in the sense that the Labour Party has tended to be.

A second point is that he was never interested in that cluster of ideas associated with the concept of 'social justice'. He just didn't believe in it. It wasn't a passion of his, he never wrote about it. For him redistribution was simply a means to obtain full employment, meaning a moderate amount of redistribution. He never had that passion for social justice which is distinctively socialist. What I think he tended to believe was simply that if you got wealth creation going

1. John Maynard Keynes as an Eton scholar in 1902.

2. Duncan Grant's drawing of John Maynard Keynes, 1908.

3. J. M. Keynes, 1926. Cartoon by David Low, *New Statesman*, 1933.

4. John Maynard Keynes in the 1930s. (*Hulton/Deutsch*)

5. (*above*) '*The lifeboat that stayed ashore*'. Cartoon by David Low, *The Evening Standard*, 1929.

6. (*below*) Maynard and Lydia Keynes in 1932. Oil painting by William Roberts.

7. 'The feller ought to be ashamed! Encouraging rain!' Cartoon by David Low, from *The Evening Standard*, 5 January 1938.

8. 'Canute shushes the waves'. Cartoon by David Low from *The Evening Standard*, 8 February 1940.

on for long enough, you would solve the problem of poverty by that means: the able people would get on and everyone would find their own level. I think it was very much that: a curious Victorian social attitude married to modern economics.

BLAUG: Looking forward now, rather than backward, do you think the Keynesian Revolution is still going on, or has it in some sense failed and come to an end?

SKIDELSKY: I don't think it has come to an end. I think at the moment that no one knows how to get it going again. That's really the problem. Even when people talk about failure, they are thinking in relative terms. I don't think the Keynesian Revolution failed, if you consider that for 20–25 years it gave the world unparalleled prosperity. The world has never enjoyed a 25-year period of such full employment and such high rates of growth. That took place under Keynesian dispensation. Let's not say that the Keynesian Revolution caused it, but it took place under governments that subscribed to Keynesian policies. So one cannot really talk about failure, and those people who say the Keynesian Revolution failed are rewriting history. The thing started to go wrong as many systems started to go wrong, really only in the 1970s, and I think in the two earlier decades it was a tremendous success story.

Nevertheless, it did start to go wrong, and one has to ask: was this some flaw in Keynes's original vision of the economic process, or was it some flaw in the application of the Keynesian message by governments? Now, I don't think that Keynes can be blamed for all that went wrong. I don't think the Keynesian Revolution as it developed fitted Keynes's view of how it ought to have developed. For one thing, I don't think Keynes would ever have been mad enough to have gone for unemployment targets of 1 or 2 per cent, as we in Britain did in the 1950s, thinking such low levels of unemployed would have no inflationary consequences. There is nothing in his writing that suggests that he ever believed that you could safely go for an unemployment target of less than 5 per cent; 5 per cent was the minimal sustainable level as far as he was concerned. So, I think policy after Keynes had very little to do with what Keynes himself would have done.

Secondly, he never believed in fiscal fine tuning, such as was practised in Britain particularly. He never believed the government budget should have that kind of responsibility for stabilising the economy. He always thought that was something monetary policy would mainly do, and monetary policy, he thought, would be much more independent of political control than fiscal policy. Quite right too.

So on those grounds I don't think it was Keynes's fault that things started to go wrong. The problem today is how to restart the Keynesian Revolution, given the position that unemployment seems to be the only way available to governments at the moment for keeping down inflation. That's really why you can't pursue full-employment policies. And that is the main area of how to keep down costs, when you are actually expanding the economy, that no one has the answer to.

BLAUG: When you talk of restarting the Keynesian Revolution, what do you really have in mind? What is the essence of the Keynesian Revolution in your view?

SKIDELSKY: I think the central message, which is absolutely valid today, is that economies aren't self-correcting. When they experience a great shock, they can run down and remain in a run-down condition for a very long period of time, and there are things governments can do about it. Governments can do what the market is supposed to do but doesn't in fact do. The validity of that message is shown by what has been happening in Britain over the last five or six years. The economy did run down; Mrs Thatcher and her ministers said: 'It will recover very soon. We just have to allow the market to have its play and we will get back very quickly to full employment.' In fact, we've had unemployment of three million or so for five or six years now. It hasn't bounced back, and the bounce-back, if it has started, has been very small. And I think many people in Britain, especially those in the middle of politics, both Conservatives of a more moderate kind than our Prime Minister and also people on the Left, do advocate a Keynesian policy, a mild form of reflation. The thing that always kills them when they do this, when they say we want demand management, is the argument that it will just rekindle the fires of inflation. And it's perfectly true. Keynesianism is politically impossible as long as unemployment is the only strategy available to keep down inflation. And that is where we have got to rethink, that's where the Keynesian Revolution needs rethinking. But I have no doubt that rethinking is going on. It's a problem that will be overcome. We will be able to restart the Keynesian Revolution, I'm absolutely sure. Furthermore, I think people who write Keynes off as a failure are very premature. He's far too considerable a twentieth-century figure to be shunted off into a side-turning labelled 'obsolete ideas'!

* * *

Paul A. Samuelson

Paul Samuelson (1915–) was the first American economist to receive the Nobel Prize in economics. He is the author of one of the seminal books of modern economics, *Foundations of Economic Analysis* (1947), as well as the most successful elementary textbook in economics ever published, *Economics: an Introductory Analysis* (1948), a book which incidentally was a major factor in the Keynesian conquest of American economics in the years after World War II.

So far I had talked around the Keynesian Revolution. Talking to Paul Samuelson at the Massachusetts Institute of Technology, I was determined to explore the question of the Keynesian Revolution more directly.

BLAUG: Professor Samuelson, in an obituary which you wrote on Keynes in 1946, you described *The General Theory* as a 'work of genius', but you said – I forget the exact words – that the book was badly put together and poorly written; in it the Keynesian system stands out only indistinctly and yet it's a work of genius. How is it that a book that in so many ways is really quite an obscure and confusing book should have hit the profession like a bombshell?

SAMUELSON: I think, first, because when something is really revolutionary and you have to work very hard to get the meat out of the shell, you think it's more important after you have performed all that work. If it had been more lucidly clear, people would have said 'Oh, yes, I knew that all along'. So I think that is part of the story.

The other part of the story is to remember that Keynes on this occasion was really talking to his colleagues at the frontier of science. The book has never been a success as a textbook. I suppose that part of my fortune is papered on Keynes's lack of success in writing a beautifully simple text-book, which we know from his writings he was perfectly capable of doing. He was addressing his peers, the cream of the cream of the profession, and they were ready to do the work to find the merit if it was there.

There were many beautiful passages in the book. For example, there is the passage in which he compares the stock market to a beauty contest: you don't even try to find the most beautiful girl, you try to find the girl whom other people will think is the most beautiful. Those passages add much to the book but its scientific success was not due to that at all. It was due to his friends in the high court. The success was due to the fact that the Great Depression, the world as it was, was calling for a new theory of economics, and Keynes was the first with the mostest. There were other people who had independent anticipations of what Keynes had, even as Charles Darwin had his Alfred Wallace. But Keynes was the one who put the new ideas on the map. He shook us up. I have put in the records how much I resisted. No Jesuit fighting against disbelief ever worked harder than I did to keep my classical convictions. I am a dodo bird sitting in front of you. I was still twenty when *The General Theory* came out, but I had a very early education. I was precocious and I was at the University of Chicago, the inner temple of classical economics. So unlike my friend Jim Tobin, who always says that he didn't know any better than to be a Keynesian because he started just after Keynes arrived, I knew what it was like before, and I know what it was like after. It was because the old theory had no handle at all to explain what was happening in London, in New York and Main Street, Iowa in the years 1930 to 1936. There was a tremendous opening here, and it was Keynes who magnificently made a beginning in filling that opening.

BLAUG: What would you say was the central message of this very complex and confusing book?

SAMUELSON: The central message was that Keynes took the level of unemployment and the level of aggregate output as a variable to be explained, whereas the schoolmen who taught me really had a theory that the only unemployment possible was a zero rate of unemployment, because a classical system can always find its equilibrium where everybody who really wants a job will be able to find one.

Now, mind you, we weren't crazy. We lived in a world where one in four people couldn't get jobs. All through my four years at college I never had a job. (I'm wrong: one Saturday afternoon I earned three dollars on a job!) But it wasn't for want of trying. I sat on the bench because I was a middle-class boy, but I had friends who would try 800 different employers with no success, so I could read the signals. We knew that there were business cycles, which were quite strong in America; we just had no theory. It was like wine tasters. You drink the white wine of pure theory from nine to ten in your classroom, then you go across the hall, you have a little cheese to clear your palate, and then you did business cycles, without any theory at all, which were taken as facts, as if facts ever tell their own story. What Keynes did was to give us a bridge between those two classrooms, the classroom of microeconomics and the classroom of macroeconomics. And you won't believe this, but the word macroeconomics did not exist. I was once accused of having invented it, and did some research and found it was not in the first edition of my textbook. It was bringing to the frontier of science the burning problem of unemployment and later inflation, which had always been in economics, that represented the Keynesian Revolution. And so if there was a Galilean Revolution, if there was a Newtonian Revolution, if there was a Maxwellian Revolution, if there was an Einstein Revolution, and maybe there was a Quantum Revolution of Max Planck, then by every objective test in the methodology, philosophy and history of science you have to say there was Keynesian Revolution.

BLAUG: Well, your textbook, *Economics: An Introductory Analysis* is of course a very important milestone in the Keynesian Revolution, because yours was one of the first books to bring Keynesian economics down to the level of the beginning students in the subject.

When you wrote that book you clearly regarded yourself as a Keynesian.

SAMUELSON: Yes.

BLAUG: Would you still regard yourself as a Keynesian today? Do you think that label has any meaning?

SAMUELSON: I regard myself as a post-Keynesian, an eclectic post-Keynesian, because I don't regard Keynesianism as a religion. I don't regard it as an ideology. I regard it as a tool of scientific research, and I actually did not like a certain note that I thought I detected at the hundredth anniversary of Keynes's birth, celebrated at the holy of holies, King's College, Cambridge. Person after person got up, walked the sawdust trail and said: 'I am just as firm a Keynesian as I ever was. I am an unreconstructed Keynesian.' And I finally exploded and said: 'We don't want unreconstructed Keynesians. We want people who will carry the scientific analysis further.' And I have to say, as kindly as I can, that in the home country of England–read the Radcliffe Report on money, published in 1959 – respected Keynesians, my friends, who in 1959 were still preaching model T, 1936 Neanderthal Keynesianism.

I am not a Neanderthal Keynesian. I am an end-of-the-century Keynesian, and I think that that's where Maynard Keynes would have been today, because you will remember that he was always accused of continually changing his mind. If a Royal Commission asked five economists for their opinion, the old joke used to be that they got six replies, two from Mr Keynes. Well, he was unrepentant when people accused him of this protean quality. He said, 'when my information changes, I change my mind. What do you do, sir?' Well, I change my mind, so I am a very different kind of Keynesian than I was. However, just as the stock market has its ups and downs, and General Motors has its time of fashion and IBM has its time, the kind of post-Keynesian eclecticism has been doing much better in the 1980s. 'Reaganomics', for example; I don't think it is a mystery how imperfectly it has worked, or how well it has worked in certain directions. I think it was a very predictable thing from the standpoint of Keynesianism fifty years on.

BLAUG: Let me take you back a minute – back to the Keynesian Revolution, I mean. There are one or two aspects of the Keynesian Revolution which continue to puzzle us when we think about it. One of them is the strange way in which the the Keynesian Revolution coincided with what one might call the 'quantitative revolution' – that is, a rise in the 1930s of econometrics, national income accounting and interest in the measurement of economic magnitudes which started a little before *The General Theory* but to which *The General Theory* gave a tremendous fillip. Can you still remember, as a young economist, feeling that by doing Keynesian economics you were at the same time helping to make economics a more quantitative, metric kind of science?

SAMUELSON: Yes, But I think you must admit the role of coincidence in the history of science. And I think that the 'mathematicisation' of economics was on its way and would have flowered if there had not been the Keynesian Revolution. I believe the Keynesian Revolution gave the mathematical theorists a new paradigm to analyse using the new tools, and the national income macro-aggregates gave the statisticians, the economic statisticians, the materials to work with. But it is actually an exaggeration – history never gets things right, you know – that Keynes himself was a great force making for the collection, tabulation and measurement of many macro-aggregates. He had an extremely modest role in that regard – not a pivotal one in the statistical revolution within the US government and at the National Bureau of Economic Research in the years just before World War II and, as the more intimate history of the British national income investigations shows, not a major one even in his own country. These two things came together nicely, but they are distinguishable. In short, Keynes was lucky. He rode on the back of horses he had not himself saddled.

BLAUG: One of the peculiar features of the Keynesian Revolution was the way Keynes was hated by the extreme Right and the extreme Left. He attracted extreme hostility from the ends of the political spectrum rather than the middle. Can you explain why it is that the Keynesian Revolution has this odd way of uniting Right and Left?

SAMUELSON: If you believed, as a good Marxist would believe in the early 1930s, that the death knell of capitalism was being sounded, that this was a system which was dying of malignancy, irreversibly on its way to a system of socialism and the withering away of the state, think how disappointed you would be if along came a middle-class Bohemian and said, 'It's just a matter of a few tricks. Print the little green paper and the dilemma of the capitalist system will be solved.' It's too easy, you would think, but also it's depriving you of what it is that you want in the timetable of history. This was in Britain in the case of people like John Strachey. I also remember it well in a measure here with the original New Dealers, who went to Washington with Franklin Roosevelt and were not communists but followers of Thorstein Veblen, who wanted a restructuring of American life. They did not like us Keynesians, who came in and began to get some power by the time of the second Roosevelt term, because we were a lightening rod which deflected their timetable of history.

It's paradoxical. Many people have said John Maynard Keynes was truly the saviour of capitalism. Remember 1932, when more than 8,000 American banks failed. Small-town editors of newspapers in the US, when polled by the National Industrial Conference Board, were in favour by a considerable majority of nationalising the banking system. That's how desperate the situation was in America, the homeland of capitalism. And fifteen years later, twenty years later, when the Keynesian Revolution had done its work, there was absolutely no danger from this quarter. So you might wonder why the Right didn't warm up to Keynes. Herbert Hoover, our emeritus President who lived a very long time as a bitter, unpopular man, never used the word 'Keynesian' without hyphenating it with 'Marxist': the 'Marxist-Keynesist doctrine, he would say, 'this nefarious doctrine'. My textbook got a magnificent start in terms of sales because a good friend of mine, a Canadian-American, Lorie Tarshis, who had been a student of Keynes, had written an excellent textbook the year before me; he was robbed of commercial success because of extreme right-wing, poisonous attacks on his book and upon him personally. By the date we are talking about, the years immediately after the war, in Britain Keynes had become a revered part of the Establishment. But in America, there was still a long way to go before Keynesianism came to be accepted in academic circles. Of course, the peak was reached at the time of Camelot, at the time of President Kennedy and President Johnson, when Walter Heller and James Tobin and Kermit Gordon, as a great team of advisors to the President, did succeed in getting the country moving, and we had more than a hundred months of uninterrupted business cycle advance, which is simply unheard of in the annals of the National Bureau of Economic Research.

What's curious to me – and history will perhaps not stop even to notice it – is that in the feckless economics of 'Reaganomics' you finally are getting from the Right a mindless form of Keynesianism. They justify by saying, 'Nothing to worry about. We will outgrow it. Growth itself will bring in new tax revenues. The Laffer Curve will take care of the problem.' (Well, they don't say that any more because it has been laughed at so much!)

Of course, they would never espouse these doctrines under the name of Keynes. In political life, in intellectual life, in ideological life, you always have to have the new Kleenex; old names get used up and you need new labels. But, nevertheless, a lot of Reaganomics is Keynesianism all over again.

BLAUG: Is there a sort of litmus-paper test that you can apply to a piece of macroeconomics to tell whether it is 'Keynesian' or 'anti-Keynesian'? What is the kernel of the argument that makes a macroeconomic assertion Keynesian rather than anti-Keynesian?

SAMUELSON: What is the acid test of whether an idea is not Keynesian? What is it that survives in the living corpus of science at the frontier after more than fifty years from the time of the Keynesian Revolution?

If in 1980 I am anti-Keynesian, I must use the language, the tools of Keynes, tools which did not even exist in economic science in the years when I began the study of economics at the University of Chicago before 1936. The theory that because wealth will pile up in the hands of people and that will reduce their savings, so that we will get out of unemployment by falling prices (that's what we call the 'Pigou Effect' after Keynes's friend and enemy Arthur C. Pigou), that 'Pigou Effect', which is a refutation of certain simple Keynesianisms, could not have been fabricated in the pre-Keynesian era. It uses the income system, the aggregates which John Maynard Keynes introduced into economics in 1936. As a scientist I could not ask for immortality than that my works are what my friends and my enemies in centuries after me need still to work with.

Let's got to what for the non-economist, the person in the street, is important about Keynesianism. I would say, first, there was the notion that in time of terrible social distress something can be done about it. We do not have to accept plague and war and lightning as Acts of God and just bow down before it, but we can do something about it. Even in the great Irish famine of the nineteenth century, at the heyday of *laissez-faire* capitalism, there was an attempt to give public works to starving people. What Keynes did was to give this generous spirit which always existed, and the political steam which in every depression exists without regard to any schoolbooks, a rational explanation of how it would work quantitatively, and what might be some of its limitations. The willingness to intervene, to lean against the wind, by the Federal Reserve central bank, by the budget of the national government – that is part and parcel of Keynesianism.

Let me mention another important respect which marks the
Keynesian, but of the 1980s as distinct from the Keynesian of the
1930s. A critic of Keynesianism like Professor Martin Feldstein at
Harvard says: 'The trouble with Keynesianism is that it is against
saving. It encourages the government to set up a social security
system so that nobody has to save, you just pay at the other end out of
taxes.'

Now that's a correct accusation for the 1930s. We deliberately
said – when I say 'we', I mean Alvin Hansen, my teacher, my friend,
who helped frame that system – it will just make the Great Depression worse if we raise taxes in order to finance social security. But
neither Hansen nor I thirty years later, to say nothing of fifty years
later, would take the view that it's a tragedy if people do more saving.
Actually, Professor Tobin and I have led a crusade for more than
twenty-five years in the Democratic Party to try and get more savings
by the US people by having a very austere budget; over-balance the
budget, but offset that by a very easy monetary policy. It is very hard
to persuade anyone on that. So that illustrates two things: what
old-fashioned, simple Keynesianism was like, but also, and I think
more importantly, how a good scientific method like the Keynesian
will adjust itself to changing circumstances, will not be frozen in
earlier frames of thought.

BLAUG: But if the Keynesian system is changing in response to
changing circumstances, to the extent that it's still Keynesian, there
must be something unchanged that remains the essence of the
Keynesian approach.

SAMUELSON: Yes, it's the method of analysis which looks for the
balance between the propensity to save at full employment and the
factors making for the propensity to invest. And in a time like
wartime, when the propensity to utilise resources is very high and the
propensity to save under *laissez-faire* would normally be the same,
John Maynard Keynes had to write a quite different kind of pamphlet, *How to Pay for the War*, in which he advocated the reverse of that
which he had been recommending to President Roosevelt at the
bottom of the Great Depression.

BLAUG: So far we have talked about the influence of Keynes, the
legacy of Keynes in the areas of economic theory and in the field of
economic policy. But let me turn for a moment to a third aspect of the
Keynesian legacy, his influence on political behaviour. Now James
Buchanan has argued that in the area of political decision-making,

Keynesian economics has left vote-conscious governments with a legacy of perpetual deficit finance; that Keynesian economics encourages governments to spend in excess of taxes, and that this has much to do with the 'inflation-proneness' of modern economies. So that one of the legacies of Keynes is to leave us with a kind of lasting tendency towards inflation. What do you think of this sort of 'public choice' argument?

SAMUELSON: I think there is an element of truth in the view that the superstition that the budget must be balanced at all times, once it is debunked, takes away one of the bulwarks that every society must have against expenditure out of control. There must be discipline in the allocation of resources or you will have anarchistic chaos and inefficiency. and one of the functions of old-fashioned religion was to scare people by what might be regarded as myths into behaving in a way that long-run civilised life requires. We have taken away a belief in the intrinsic necessity of balancing the budget – if not every year, in every short period of time. If Prime Minister Gladstone came back to life he would say, 'Oh, oh, oh, what have you done?', and James Buchanan argues in those terms.

I have to say that I see merit in that view, nowhere more than in connection with Reaganomics. What we are having now is a case, not of wild left-wing plans being financed out of the residue of this new licentious freedom, but rather military expenditures, tax reductions; so that in my view the United States has been selling the farm to the Japanese, to the Pacific Basin, to certain surplus continental countries.

My hope has always been to replace irrational disciplines by rational disciplines, that one should understand why Buchanan thinks it's an evil that these results should have taken place, and to build into our educated college population – my constituency, my responsibility as a teacher – an understanding of wherein lies the evil of the structural deficit of Reaganomics, and where that evil of a structural deficit – I am using old fashioned language – differs from the virtue of a cyclical deficit of the kind that in Kennedy's Camelot was prescribed by the economic experts.

There is nothing inconsistent about being in favour of a deficit then and against it now. If Herbert Hoover had asked me as a school kid to advise, I would have told him that he should not be trying to raise taxes in the midst of a crash and a depression. He should be deliberately contriving a therapeutic deficit. But I would say exactly the opposite to Ronald Reagan. So there is the difference. Now I happen to believe that, if I may paraphrase, learn the truth and the truth will help make you free and maybe even efficient.

* * *

James Tobin

James Tobin (1918–   ) is America's most distinguished Keynesian. His lifetime's work on monetary economics in the Keynesian mould earned him the Nobel Prize in economics in 1981.

The leading Keynesian economist of the older generation is not Paul Samuelson but James Tobin. He decided to study economics in 1936, and *The General Theory* was in fact the first book that he read on economics at Yale University. It made a deep impression on him. When I spoke to him at Yale University, I asked him why it had made such an impact on him.

_____

TOBIN: I was a sophomore at Harvard College, just beginning to study economics. My tutor gave me Keynes's new book, saying: 'They tell me it might be important.' So I read *The General Theory*. It was the first serious economics book I read. I did that because this young man, who was my tutor, didn't know that I was too young to read such a book and too inexperienced. Why did it make such an impression on a nineteen-year-old in 1936? Well, because anybody alert to world problems was distressed by the economic and political problems of the day and the apparent inability of anybody to do anything about them. And here was a book that logically said what to do, what could be done. It wasn't hopeless. And it also said it in a way that was exciting to a student who was mathematically, theoretically and quantitatively inclined. You like theoretical controversy when you are that age. You like the good guys and the bad guys, and side with the forces of new thought against the encrusted orthodoxy, and it appealed to me that I could join the revolt against it.

BLAUG: You said one of the things that was exciting about *The General Theory* was that it appeared to offer some ways of dealing with the depression of the 1930s. Yet one of the odd things about this book is that it is almost entirely theoretical and only starts talking about policy in the closing pages, and then in a most general way. It doesn't even advocate in its closing pages anything like deficit finance, which is what is usually associated with Keynesian policy. So the perplexing thing about the book is why such an abstract book on economic theory should have been thought to be relevant to the depression of the 1930s?

TOBIN: Well, *The General Theory* is an abstract book about economic theory, but it cleared the way for people to come along with anti-depression policies; such views were now respectable and not the works of cranks who did not understand economics. You couldn't say that any more after Keynes brought out *The General Theory* and exposed, well, the bankruptcy of standard neo-classical theory, which had no explanation of 25 per cent unemployment and no remedy for it either.

There were a lot of people who favoured, on pragmatic grounds, public works and other commonsense remedies for unemployment. What Keynes did was to provide a logical argument to oppose the

standard arguments against such measures, which said they were
inflationary, they wouldn't do any good, they would just crowd out
other jobs.

In the United States people rushed in pretty quickly with the
lessons of Keynesian theory for policy. It is true that in the book itself
there was not much about fiscal policy and exploiting the multiplier
for public works. But Alvin Hansen came to Harvard in 1936, and
immediately the brains of young graduate students and faculty were
enrolled in the economics of fiscal policy following Keynesian lines.

BLAUG: How would you sum up the central message of Keynesian
economics? *The General Theory* is full of all sorts of strands and
ideas. Is there a central message?

TOBIN: The central message of *The General Theory* is pretty clear, I
think. It's given in the first part of *The General Theory*. It is that you
cannot rely on the free market to maintain full-employment equilibrium. The self-recuperating, self-adjusting features of the system are
too weak to do that. Contrary to the neoclassical belief that any time
a market is out of balance, then price movements will put it back into
equality of supply and demand, Keynes came along and said that may
be true of the fish market or the market for rice, but it is not true of
the national or international market for goods and services in total.

BLAUG: Well, was there a central theoretical concept among the
many that he employed, would you say?

TOBIN: Yes, I think there was. There was the concept of effective
demand. It was a central concept introduced by Keynes early in the
book. Effective demand as opposed to hypothetical or sometimes
later called 'notional demand'. The idea is pretty simple. If
unemployed people don't get work and don't get paid, then you
cannot expect them to buy the same quantities of consumer goods
that they would buy if they had jobs and got paid. Whereas
neoclassical theory tended to stick with the ideas that demands were
based on how much you wanted to sell in the market, not how much
you actually did sell. Keynes said that doesn't make sense. Obviously, the demand of workers will be constrained by how much
labour they are able to sell. Therefore, the receipts of employers will
be constrained by how much they are able to sell in the market, and
there will be a general failure of co-ordination. It won't solve itself if
left alone. That opens the door for policy intervention. But it opens
the door for policy intervention of a pretty simple kind. We must
remember that we are talking about the 1930s, when there were all

these foreboding doomsday books about capitalism and democracy, saying that the Great Depression proves these systems don't work and they will have to go on the scrap heap of history. So along comes Keynes and says the system could work just fine – you just have to know which buttons to push and which levers to pull.

BLAUG: Is this one of the reasons why Keynes invited, and to some extent still invites, hostility from the extreme Right and the extreme Left – in the sense that he said not only that the economy is sick, but also that we can find a doctor who can cure it?

TOBIN: It's a remarkable fact that Keynes is hated by leftists and rightists both. I think the reason is the same in both cases: that Keynesian economics says that the system, the kind of mixed economy, democratic, capitalist/socialist system that we have got in this country and in Europe and Japan, that the system is very robust and can work even under the burdens of considerable taxation for various purposes. It can work with the welfare state. It can work with progressive taxation. It's not full of contradictions which doom it to revolution or collapse. Both the rightists and the leftists think that the only way a capitalist system can work is by severe inequality of income and wealth. That's what the 'supply-siders' say nowadays. That's the only way to make the system work and that's what the leftists have always said: 'it's got to be cruel or it won't work'. So they are both saying the same thing, and the Keynesian analysis comes down to the middle and says you don't have to be that pessimistic about it.

BLAUG: A part of the impact of Keynes and part of the reason why Keynesian economics succeeded so quickly and so massively was the fact that Keynes seemed to operate with variables that he always tried to make operational, or at least capable of being measured quantitatively, and in this way he held out the hope that economics could become a much more quantitative science than it had ever been. What has been called the quantitative revolution and the Keynesian Revolution sort of went hand in hand, I think, in the 1930s. Was that a coincidence?

TOBIN: It was a very fortunate coincidence that the development of national income accounting was reaching a viable state at the same time that *The General Theory* came along. The reason there was good luck, mutual good luck, was that the Keynesian theory's variables – consumption, saving and investment, income, etc. – were beginning to be measured. And the national income accountants probably never thought that they would have a theory that would be such an obvious and fertile place to use the accounts they were producing and estimating both in this country and in Britain. It's ironic, too, because Keynes was not very enchanted with fancy quantitative work in economics. He wasn't enchanted with Tinbergen's work, for example, in econometrics, in trying to build an empirical, statistical model with real numbers in it, a numerical model of exactly the Keynesian system. Keynes liked tables, obvious ways of presenting statistics, and he rather thought that multiple regressions and other things that the statisticians do were some kind of black box magic. There were three things: there was Keynesian theory; there was the coming of age of national income accounting; and there was the development of econometric methods, and they all converged to a very happy combination.

BLAUG: Keynes died in 1946. That started what has been called 'The Age of Keynes', the twenty-five years of relative prosperity – indeed, an unprecedented period of prosperity in the history of capitalism, which many people attribute to the adoption by governments in every industrialised country in the world of Keynesian demand management, Keynesian fine tuning. Many people regard this as proof of the validity of Keynesian economics. Do you think this is a valid argument?

TOBIN: The first quarter-century after the Second World War was a period of unparalleled growth and prosperity in the non-communist, industrial, developed countries and in their trade with each other. I think it's true that most of all countries, the United States and the United Kingdom, for sure, had resolved that they were not going to undergo the Great Depression again. There was a lot of fear that after the war ended and there was demobilisation, especially in the United States, that we would revert to the pre-war 1930s depression. There was a lot of fear about that, and we passed the Employment Act of 1946, which put on paper a resolution of the Congress and the country that we would use the powers of the Federal Government, 'To maintain maximum employment, production and purchasing power'. That's what the Act says, and the Council of Economic Advisers and other machinery, the Economic Report of the President required every year – that was all set up as a result of the Act. It institutionalised Keynesian accounting for the economy, and at least to some degree it assigned the responsibility. It was already a Keynesian thing to do. It assigned the responsibility for the outcome in terms of national income and employment to the Federal Government. That was not regarded as a responsiblity of the Federal Government by all the people in the 1930s or the 1920s, but in the 1950s and 1960s almost every administration in the United States used Keynesian policies and was expected to use Keynesian policies – Truman, Eisenhower, Kennedy, Johnson – some more than others, some more publicly than others; some just did it without making a point of doing so, but they did it and it was a very different policy from what was followed in the twenties and early thirties.

BLAUG: But was that prosperity due to these Keynesian policies that the American government was undoubtedly pursuing, or was it merely happenchance, good luck? There were so many other reasons why consumption spending was very high, and similarly why investment spending was very high. That is, it is one thing to say the American government adopted Keynesian policies, and it's another thing to say 'and therefore it was the adoption of these correct policies that produced the prosperity'.

TOBIN: Well, it's always a question in interpreting any historical period, and it is always hard to say that these events are due to one factor or another. That is the problem of economic history – in fact of all history, all kind of history. I think that our policies had a lot to do with it. The change in the mental state of the public, of the ordinary civil servant, politicians, journalists had a lot to do with the acceptability of the policies that were followed in this country until . . . well, almost until now. We never had a break until a new Administration came in 1981 which consciously rejected Keynesian economics, but that doesn't mean they haven't used Keynesian remedies. Intellectually, ideologically, they have said it's bad and we are against it.

BLAUG: And yet here is the paradox of the Reagan Administration, which is explicitly anti-Keynesian, operates a large budgetary deficit, and in Britain many economists say, 'Ah, the reason why America has lower unemployment than Britain is because America has a budgetary deficit whereas Britain doesn't'.

TOBIN: History is full of ironies. The fact that the Reagan Administration ran a massive deficit, much higher than an explicitly Keynesian administration would ever have wanted to do – that is an ultimate irony. We should not in the United States anyway attach a Keynesian label to simple running of deficits. That's a canard, and it's myth in the public view of what Keynesian economics is.

During the 1940s – late '40s and '50s – there was in this country a kind of synthesis of the older ideas of orthodox theory, sometimes called neo-classical theory, and Keynesian theory. Paul Samuelson at

MIT was one of the main motive forces of this development. This synthesis did not say, 'always run deficits and spend money for fiscal policy'. It wasn't that. First of all it gave a co-equal status to monetary policy, the policy of the central bank, the Federal Reserve System. Since we could use more than one policy to stabilise the economy and to maintain full employment, we ought to worry about which mixture of the two policies we should use.

It's as if you have two medicines. They both will cure you and they will have, however, different side effects. OK, your doctor ought to think about in what 'mix' you should take the two medicines. The same is true of monetary and fiscal policy. So with the doctrine of neo-Keynesian economists in the United States in the 1950s and 1960s. They held that you shouldn't run great big deficits and then have to have a tight monetary policy in order to restrain the economy from over-stimulation by the big deficits. They tried to be in the middle of the road, or, if anything, have a tighter budget and make up for it by having lower interest rates and easier money, because that's good for the growth of the economy. The Reagan Administration did just the opposite. We could have had the same recovery in the United States in the '80s with pre-Reagan fiscal policies; then we would have had easier money, lower interest rates and we would have the same recovery. We wouldn't have a vast public debt growing, and vast international debt growing.

BLAUG: In the last ten or fifteen years, Keynesian macroeconomics was succeeded for a while by the monetarist counter-revolution. That was succeeded to some extent by the new classical macroeconomics. At the moment it's anybody's guess, I suppose, which has the upper hand, but there are still many macroeconomists like yourself who would describe themselves as Keynesian, neo-Keynesians. Now what is it that makes macroeconomics Keynesian rather than anti-Keynesian or neo-Keynesian?

TOBIN: I am still glad to be called a Keynesian. In fact, I am more willing to be described that way because of the extremes on the other side that have arisen in recent years. It's a thing to be proud of. Originally I didn't like to be labelled at all. You know, we are economists. We are trying to do our best to understand the world, and we don't have to be labelled in schools. But the way things have turned out, you can't avoid it now. What is the major issue between Keynesians, old and young – there really are some young ones coming along – what's the major issue between us and the New Classical Economists? It's the same as between Keynes and his opponents in the 1930s. It's whether there is a reliable mechanism that will keep the economy on the full-employment track without government policy to help maintain it in that position. The people Keynes was opposing – the 'Treasury view' and all that – in the 1930s in Britain thought there was a reliable mechanism. The conservative economists of our profession here in the United States think there is now. And it's the same position. They have new ammunition, but not any new empirical ammunition. In fact, all the empirical investigations are still supporting Keynesian views. What they have is a theory which more economists of the present day are inclined to believe on presumptive, logical grounds – not because they have persuasive empirical grounds. It's the old Invisible Hand theory that goes back to Adam Smith: Left to themselves, people will act in their own interests. Competitive markets will magically transmute their self-interests into the general welfare. Now that was never applied in macroeconomics *per se* as a presumptive truth until the last fifteen years, but now it has become so with the new theory of rational expectations. It puts a burden of proof on Keynes and on others: if you think the market has failed that much, you have a major burden of explaining how such a thing could possibly happen.

I notice that more and more young economists, bright young economists, are turned off by the failure of this simplistic Panglossian theory to explain the facts, and so they are working hard to explain the facts, but they are not going to shut their eyes to the facts so they may use some new methodology. After all, there is technical progress even in our profession, but they will be part of a still new Keynesian movement. That's as it should be, but the Keynesian critique of the free market ideology will stand. It will just be buttressed by new ways of thinking about it.

BLAUG: So what, summarising it, endures of Keynes? Is it simply the critique of what you call free market ideology or the self-recuperative powers of the market economy? Is it simply that that endures or is it more than that? Is it an apparatus of thought? Is it a set of concepts? Are things like the consumption function, the multiplier, the definitions of saving and investment and so on the Keynesian view of the labour market? Do such concepts still survive?

TOBIN: Yes, I think the basic message of *The General Theory* will survive, and so also will lots of the specific concepts, functions and relationships. They do. They are part of the vocabulary the students learn and economists use. Even those who have never read the book are using those ideas. So liquidity preference, marginal efficiency of learn and that economists use. Even those who have never read the book are using those ideas. So liquidity preference, marginal efficiency of investment, all those tools – we don't need to go into them – sure, they are still part of the vocabulary of the understanding of economists. The pages of *The General Theory* contain almost all the ideas on the same subjects that people have had in the intervening fifty-odd years. At least there are hints of them and evidence that Keynes thought about them; a lot can be found in there that's not systematised, but it does show what a good economist Keynes was. But the major message is still in the labour market theory about what are the sources of the failure of markets to work as well as they could and the idea of effective demand; those are the basic, important theoretical innovations in *The General Theory*.

There is another issue, a big methodological issue in which Keynes is on one side (interestingly enough on the same side as Frank Knight of the University of Chicago, who was an economist of very different ideas about policy and the world than Keynes) against all of the methodology of the profession clearly regarded as the way to do things in economics today, that is, the modelling of uncertainty. Keynes and Knight say it is intrinsically impossible for individuals to have a rational policy with respect to the uncertainties of long-term investments and so on because those are not subject to the laws of probability that govern rolls of dice and the drawing of balls out of urns. Whereas the basically modern methodology of economics is to assume everything can be put into probabilistic terms and rational decisions about how to deal, even if it's a venture which won't pay off until a hundred years from now. Now that's a big difference which is still to be worked out in the social sciences. That's a problem that Keynes bequeathed to us.

*   *   *

Frank Hahn

(Photo: Dorothy Hahn)

Frank Hahn (1925–) is a specialist in general equilibrium theory, a highly technical branch of mathematical economics which investigates the abstract properties of multimarket equilibrium. Nevertheless, Hahn has always taken an interest in policy issues. If Tobin has been America's most outspoken opponent of 'monetarism', Hahn has probably been Britain's principal opponent. He teaches at Cambridge University, although not at the same college where Keynes taught.

Having spoken to two leading American economists about Keynes, I thought it was time to cross the Atlantic to talk to Frank Hahn. Frank Hahn is a major exponent of general equilibrium theory, and some would say that general equilibrium theory does not marry very well with Keynesian macroeconomics.

BLAUG: Professor Hahn, you once said that Keynes had a 'poet's intuition and a practical man's grasp, but he did not begin to know how to theorise rigorously'. How is it that a man who did not know how to theorise rigorously could have had such a dramatic impact on modern economics?

HAHN: Well, this question falls into two parts. That Keynes had a great intuition about the economy is clear in everything he wrote. He was himself practically involved in many spheres, in the City and in the Treasury and all sorts of other places, and he had a real understanding of what practical economics was about. So he has a great intuition, there is no question about that.

That he was not rigorous in his theorising is simply a consequence of a fact that I think he wasn't too much interested in economic theory. His teacher was Marshall, and Marshall was a man who, as it were, produced the dominant theory of the market economy, not only for England but for the Western world of that period. He codified. A great deal had gone before but he was a dominant influence. Keynes never liberated himself from what he had learned from Marshall, and yet what he had to say in the book was the plain opposite to what Marshall had to say. And that is why the book, when it appeared, was reviewed in a very hostile manner by Pigou. And the essence of that whole criticism is that here was a body of theory which said indeed, as people say now, that the market will see to it that unemployment of a large kind cannot occur. It is self-regulating essentially, and Keynes took very little trouble really to meet the challenge and say why it might not be self-regulating. Except in one respect, and that is in the attention he paid to expectations in the role of economic action when people make decisions.

Now, why was the book so influential in spite of this? Well, first of all, most readers were not economic theorists, and my guess is that many people were Keynesians without having read Keynes. What appeared was just like in Marx's *Das Kapital*; there appeared to be truly scientific diagnoses of what was wrong and a truly scientific prescription of what to do about it. That had enormous impact, obviously. Keynes's interview with Roosevelt is well known. He simply, at the right moment, produced answers which appeared to be scientific and right.

BLAUG: Yet the paradoxical thing is that *The General Theory* was a book which was almost wholly about economic theory and only in its last ten or fifteen pages turned to the questions of what to do about policy. And even then, even in those last ten or fifteen pages, it was very obscure about precisely what was being recommended, which makes it even stranger that he has that reputation of having provided a solution to the unemployment of the 1930s.

HAHN: There are several answers to that question. First of all, can a book of pure theory, more or less, be practically influential? Well, all I have to do is to refer you to Marx. Practical people often make this mistake and Keynes, of course, made a very famous remark about it that 'practical people are enslaved by "academic scribblers" (I think he called them) of previous generations'. That now counts as common sense. I think the fact that it was theoretical and difficult to understand, most people obviously didn't read it and didn't understand it, actually was a plus, because what it said here was an arcane piece of knowledge which nonetheless was going to show what a capitalist economy was really like.

As for the fact that *The General Theory* actually contained little policy, you forget, I think, that Keynes wrote a great deal besides. Keynes wrote a large number of popular articles. He was, I think, a regular correspondent in the *Manchester Guardian*. He wrote pamphlets, so he advocated policies that he could always say in the back, 'There is a scientific work of mine which tells you why I am saying such and such'.

BLAUG: Do you think there was a central message in the book? Earlier you mentioned the emphasis on expectations. Would you say that that was the central message of the book?

HAHN: It's difficult to give an unqualified 'yes'. The central message of the book to theorists was, in the first instance, to raise doubts about the Marshallian picture of a well-functioning market mechanism. In the second place, it is expectations, yes. And this is, of course, at the centre of current concerns in macroeconomics. That is, when a person takes actions which are important, such as investment in industry, buying a house, choosing an occupation, he has to attempt to say something about the future. Both the short-run future and the long-run future are important. And Keynes realised that in some sense the present 'hung by the bootstraps' of people's expectations about the future; that people's expectations about the future may have nothing whatsoever to do with what actually happens.

Now, can I just give you an example of this phenomenon? Nowadays we have shown that if people believe that sunspots have economic effects, then they will have economic effects, and, moreover, as a result we can get cyclical behaviour. We can show that the cyclical behaviour can result from these beliefs in sunspots being important. And that is a typical example of what Keynes called a 'bootstrap' situation. A person hangs by the bootstraps of his expectations.

BLAUG: But what about some theoretical concepts that he appeared to imply as central to his argument, like the consumption function, the multiplier, liquidity preference, theory of interest, etc.? Do you think that those were really central concepts of the argument or incidental to the argument?

HAHN: I think they were incidental. You mustn't forget a thing I think I took for granted in my previous answer when you asked me about the 'central point'. Keynes invented macroeconomics. That is to say, he invented theorising about aggregates – like total consumption, total investment, total income. For instance, it was Keynes who gave rise afterwards to national income accounting. That was Keynes-inspired.

Now, for this macroeconomics Keynes had to invent his own tools. All these tools had flaws in them which refer back to what we discussed earlier. Take, for instance, the consumption function. Keynes argued first of all that people's consumption was determined by their income, and secondly that as they got richer the proportion of income consumed would fall and the proportion saved would rise. He also assumed that nobody would over-consume the whole of his income; the marginal propensity to consume wouldn't be one. Well subsequent research, empirical and other, has shown that almost all of these statements are flawed. And the reason they are flawed is because Keynes made no attempt to derive what people's consumption decisions might be from a real theory of individual behaviour. What he did was to use his intuition to construct plausible arguments. Nonetheless, the concepts are now, as it were, 'in the subject' and are used in the subject. And as I said, he invented macroeconomics; everywhere where macroeconomics is done, these concepts play a role.

BLAUG: Well, let's turn now to what some people have called the 'Age of Keynes'. That is, Keynes died in 1946, and the 1950s and 1960s were periods of unprecedented prosperity in the Western world, which many people attribute to the assumption on the part of governments of Keynesian demand management and Keynesian fiscal policy. In what sense can one assign the prosperity of that entire twenty-five-year period to Keynesian demand management?

HAHN: Is the economic history of the '50s and '60s in the Western industrialised world evidence in favour of Keynesian theory? The answer is 'no'. In order to get evidence for the theory in economics you have to go through a large, difficult, complicated piece of reasoning and research, and it hasn't been done in this case. In fact, to be honest, it has been done in hardly any cases. There are very few economic theories which we can say that they have been verified or falsified by facts. However, it is true that during that period, for instance in England, we had one and a half per cent unemployment and a low inflation rate, and to that extent, while it doesn't prove that Keynes was right, it disproves those (for instance, Mrs Thatcher) who claim that government policies of the kind then pursued are bound to be inflationary.

BLAUG: Now everything changed very radically in the 1970s with the oil crisis. Industrialised economies became inflation-prone. This contributed to a belief that Keynesian economics was either always invalid or now invalid. In addition, the rise in economic theory of monetarism and the new classical macroeconomics suggested that Keynesian economics was dead or no longer relevant. That raises the question of what it is about Keynesian economics that still endures, if any of it endures. What do you think of that?

HAHN: I am tempted to answer the first part of your question of whether in fact the inflationary experiences we have had since the oil crisis have in some sense damaged the Keynesian position. I don't believe they have. But I think I will concentrate my answer on the question of whether or not it still has a role to play. I would like to say, categorically as it were, without being able to argue it here, that the proponents of neoclassical macroeconomics are in full retreat. I am happy to explain why that is the case, but I insist that it is the case. The Keynesian influence is now really at the forefront. For instance, the other day I heard Professor Sargeant, who is one of the architects of neoclassical macroeconomics, give a very good paper which was really Keynesian in spirit, because it was concerned with people's expectation formation – how people learn and how their expectation formation can in fact have profound effects on the development of an economy. So I think that the Keynesian influence is alive and well. There is an ongoing dispute, for instance now, over the notion which Keynesianism introduced of 'involuntary unemployment'. That is to say, there are people who are willing to work at the going wage but cannot find jobs, and the neoclassical economist is inclined to say, 'no, at any moment of time, people who are unemployed have chosen to be so'. I think that particular argument is in the process of being decided in favour of Keynes – namely, that periods of involuntary unemployment are perfectly possible in capitalist economies.

BLAUG: So you are suggesting there is a resurgence of Keynesian economics?

HAHN: Yes, Keynesian economics is very, very relevant, but I would like to come back to your very first question. It is not the Keynes of his book. It is not the Keynes who, as it were, was rather cavalier about all the deep theoretical issues. And what neoclassical economists have done is to say 'look, there is one theory of a market economy and it can't be too different a theory which tells you what the future incomes are going to be or what to do about unemployment'. Those two are the same object of study, and 'neo-Keynesians' are now, I think, quite determined to approach macro-problems from that point of view; that is, to integrate it into microeconomics. We want to have economic theory as an undivided whole instead of having a schizophrenic subject.

BLAUG: In a period when macroeconomists argue with one another – some are Keynesian or neo-Keynesian, some are anti-Keynesian, some monetarist – what is the litmus-paper test of an economic argument being Keynesian? Now it can't be that it involves expectations, because that's everybody's game; monetarists use arguments about expectations and the new classical macroeconomics, of course, uses notions of rational expectations, so apparently everyone has taken on board the importance of expectations. But that only raises the question of what makes a particular macroeconomic argument Keynesian rather than something else?

HAHN: All right, what makes an argument Keynesian is the following: let me come back to involuntary unemployment. Involuntary unemployment would mean that at the market wage there are people willing to work and they cannot find jobs. Another way of saying it is that at that market wage supply is not equal to demand. That possibility, that for long periods markets may be out of equilibrium because prices don't adjust – in this case money wages don't adjust – is a hallmark of Keynesian theorising. Secondly, the expectation question is of crucial importance. The neoclassical economists believe that expectations are about fundamentals: technology, tastes, crops, real things in the economy. But Keynes believed that expectations may be about quite crazy things: for instance, yesterday Wall Street fell by 9 per cent. It cannot be reconciled with a notion of rational expectations because in a rational expectation world everybody has correctly, except for a little of what we call 'white noise', anticipated the future. And Keynes was very insistent on mistakes. It is not just expectations. It is how important mistakes can be for the present.

BLAUG: So Keynes denied that expectations are necessarily rational. On the contrary, they are frequently irrational or at least inconsistent or full of errors?

HAHN: Yes, and I want to add to that. Expectations can be mistaken. What is important is that the new neoclassical macroeconomics deduced that policy is impotent. The government can do nothing to improve an economy. And as I said before, an intervention would simply lead to inflation. It is a hallmark of the Keynesian influence that many of us believe that to be false. Now when we say 'believe', I mean we argue it. And I ought to just ask, 'how do economists debate?' It isn't really that people call themselves Keynesians or neoclassical economists – at least I don't call myself any of these things – it is that you produce what you call a 'model'. For instance, Solow and I are working on a book together and we have produced a model of an economy which has all the neoclassical features, namely clearing of markets, correct expectations, but it does not lead to neoclassical results. For instance, there are many what we call 'equilibria' – that is to say, there are many possible outcomes.

The world isn't uniquely described by the neoclassical story, and we show the other side, if you like, and then we argue about it. The normal argument would be 'yes, but the assumption here isn't quite right, and so on and so forth. And that's how argument proceeds, but that Keynes is present is clear.

BLAUG: Would you object to the label 'Keynesian' being hung on you? I mean, do you object to the idea of economists choosing schools?

HAHN: Yes, very much. I think the existence of 'schools' is a sign that a subject is vastly immature or that it isn't a subject at all. That sounds pretty strong when you think of philosophers, for instance. But when you think of philosophers, the schools appear very largely in the metaphysical realm. You know, disputes about metaphysics, those are subjects which simply are not resolvable. Now economics isn't like that. Economics is a subject in which we can make our argument sufficiently precise, so that we understand each other and the dispute comes down to a questioning of facts. Now I have already said that facts are very difficult to establish in economics. Therefore, experiments. But it is not true that we are schools that just yell at each other.

BLAUG: But on the other hand, you would not object to describing yourself as someone who continues to be inspired by the vision and message of Keynes, although certainly not the details of Keynes's argument?

HAHN: Absolutely. Keynes is one of my heroes. I don't mean as a person but as an economist. Certainly he has inspired me, and I think that he continues to inspire people on all sides. It's far too early to say he is 'dead' in any way.

*   *   *

Milton Friedman

There is only one economist alive today whose name may be said to be a household word and of whom one can truly say 'he needs no introduction', and that is Milton Friedman (1912–). Now retired from academic life but for years a leading figure at the University of Chicago, he keeps himself in the public limelight on television and in the pages of newsapers. He won the Nobel Prize for economics in 1976.

The last economist I spoke to about Keynes, at the Hoover Institution, was Milton Friedman, the father of monetarism, the most prominent opponent of Keynes in macroeconomics, and the leading advocate of market-orientated, free enterprise and microeconomic policies.

BLAUG:　Professor Friedman, you have written the following statement about *The General Theory*: 'Had *The General Theory* never have been written, Keynes would nevertheless have deservedly been regarded as one of the greatest economists.' And yet, on other occasions, you have expressed disagreements of all sorts with John Maynard Keynes and his ideas. Can you explain how you can disagree with him on so many scores and yet at the same time regard him as one of the greatest economists that ever lived?

FRIEDMAN:　In my opinion, the best thing he ever wrote was a book he published in 1923 called *A Tract on Monetary Reform*. Moreover, with respect to *The General Theory* itself, I regard it as a great book but as a highly unsuccessful experiment. As you know, the road to scientific knowledge is paved with unsuccessful experiments. Most experiments are unsuccessful. The quality of a man as a scientist is not really to be judged by whether all his experiments turn out to be successful but by the kind of understanding and ingenuity that goes into his experiments, some of which turn out to be unsuccessful. In this respect, I have always thought that Keynes's theory, the theory that he called 'a general theory' in the book you referred to, was the right kind of theory. It tried to explain an apparent discrepancy in evidence that was not consistent with earlier theories. It tried to explain it by stripping things down to their essentials, to a few key elements, and seeing how much you could explain with those. It was a very ingenious experiment but it didn't work. Subsequent events did not conform to the predictions that could be derived from the theory. And therefore the theory has to be rejected, and by now has been rejected. Nobody accepts any more the 'theory' that Keynes developed in *The General Theory*.

BLAUG:　Can you say a little something about the 'theory', or at least extract from it its central message.

FRIEDMAN:　The central message of Keynes' *General Theory*, the theory he called the general theory, was that the economy was driven by investment, that consumers were a relatively passive element in the situation; that monetary factors played a relatively minor role; that the key, dynamic element in the system that drove it was investment. Now that was a great contrast, a real break with the prior economic theory which stressed that investment and consumption played a comparable role; that there is a certain level of output; people decide how to break it down between consumption and saving, and the counterpart of saving is investment; that if there were more savings, there would be more investment. 'Ah', but Keynes said, 'you have got that backwards. If there is more investment, there will be more saving. Investment is what drives it.'

In addition, the prior theory had put major emphasis on monetary factors – what happened to the quantity of money, what happened to credit conditions, and so on. Again, Keynes said, 'Those are passive elements. They will follow what happens to the level of investment and they are not dynamic elements.' In that sense money does not really matter very much. What matters is only, or primarily, investment.

As I say, this was a very fine theory, nothing wrong with it on a theoretical level, but the facts didn't accord with it. I shouldn't say the facts didn't accord with it. The predictions that could be drawn from it were not confirmed by the evidence.

BLAUG: And yet this book attracted assent from the profession, at first from young people, eventually from virtually everyone within, let us say, ten years of publication. Between *The General Theory* in 1936 and his death in 1946, within ten years, that theory conquered the economics profession all over the world. This is the so-called 'Keynesian Revolution', which at least for its speed and comprehensiveness has perhaps no precedents in the history of economic thought; no other theory ever conquered so quickly.

FRIEDMAN: I won't go into the question of whether any other theory did, but you are no doubt right that the Keynesian theory did conquer a very large fraction of the profession. Why? I think the answer is very straightforward. First, Keynes was not alone in believing that the Great Depression, the fact that you had millions and millions of people idle while you also had factories idle in which they could have worked was inconsistent with the prior body of economic thinking. It really wasn't, but it appeared to be. And there was an overwhelming demand, after all, for two things: how do we explain this phenomenon, and how do we do something about it? How do we get out of the mess we are in? Keynes's theory had three features that I think contributed to its success. First, it seemed to provide an explanation for the Great Depression to many people, although he himself did not intend it as a theory of the Great Depression. He intended it, as he said, as a 'general theory', but to many people its great appeal was, 'ah, we have got some kind of intellectually respectable explanation'.

The second thing is – and this is a little more complicated to point out – it was in a certain way a very simple theory and yet it was clothed in jargon – multiplier, propensities, accelerators – it was clothed in jargon which seemed to make it a sophisticated theory and was somewhat difficult to understand; but once understood, it was a simple machine to work. You plugged in a couple of numbers and tuned the machine and out came your answer. So it had the attractive feature that it enabled people, especially younger economists, to command what was regarded as a sophisticated body of theory, which their elders were not familiar with but which they could work easily. The elders were accustomed to dealing in other terms, and so the young were able – I was an exception because I was young at the time – to have a feeling of superiority over their elders which the young always want to do, thank God.

The third feature which appealed to people was that it seemed to be a prescription that every politician in the world loved. Every politician wants to have an excuse for spending someone else's money. I shouldn't say every politician. We would all like to have an excuse for spending other people's money, but only the politicians are in a position to do so. And here, all of a sudden, was an intellectually respectable defence of a policy which enabled them to spend other people's money without appearing to impose taxes in order to do so. It gave an intellectually respectable case for deficit spending, which was a godsend to politicians. So it was a very attractive package. And one other thing, at the time in the 1940s and early '50s, there was no alternative. In politics they say you can't beat a candidate without a candidate. Now the only alternative was what was widely regarded, although erroneously, as an outdated, antediluvian theory, which had been contradicted by the evidence of the Great Depression. And that is why I think it conquered the profession so rapidly. And not only the profession. Here you had lots of laymen outside of economics, people who were not economists, who for years had been saying, 'There must be a flaw in the price system, somehow or other things don't work the way these darned economists say it works'. And here came a highly respected economist, highest professional standing, who all of a sudden seemed to say, 'By God, you people are right. You are correct.' And so he was very popular among the so-called progressives and reformers outside the system.

BLAUG: Those were some of the ingredients for the success of Keynesian economics, but of course Keynes died in 1946, and now we come to the twenty-five years after his death, the twenty-five-year post-war period of a relatively recession-free prosperity throughout the industrialised world, which many people attributed to the assumption on the part of governments of Keynesian monetary and fiscal policies. The theory had conquered the economics profession, but now it proceeded to conquer the entire spectrum of intellectual opinion. Now can one really attribute the relative prosperity of the '50s and '60s to the success of Keynesian demand management on the part of governments?

FRIEDMAN: To that the answer is clearly 'no'. There was no such Keynesian demand management, at least not explicitly, in the prosperous '20s, and the '20s were a highly prosperous period. There was no such Keynes money management, goodness knows, in the United States in the period after the Civil War, but the period of the 1870s and 1880s was a period of very rapid growth in the United States. The '50s and '60s, viewed objectively, were very good years, don't misunderstand me, but they were no more impressive than the 1865–1885 period. They were no more impressive than the 1920s. I don't believe you can attribute the relative world prosperity of the period to Keynesian demand management. It's not entirely clear what you can attribute it to. My view has always been a very simple one: the most important thing is to avoid major mistakes in policy; that the really catastrophic periods like the Great Depression were caused by mistakes. It's not so much that government has the propensity to do things, but that it has the propensity to wreck things. And I believe we were very lucky in the '50s and '60s that there were no major mistakes of that kind. You notice it is not an accident that the other periods I mentioned are periods after great wars, because a period after a war is inevitably a period in which you have fallen behind on a great many things and when there are unsatisfied demands, in which there tends to be relative prosperity.

But I want to go back to another aspect of your question. You say that the policies of the '50s and '60s gave the final cachet to the success of Keynes. Remember that the people who were in charge of policy and, more important, the people who were in charge of interpreting policy and its performance were these young people who were captivated; these were people who had been young in the '30s and '40s, young economists who had been captivated by Keynes, who had become Keynesian, and they were the people who were now writing all the discussions of what was going on. Whether the policy was Keynesian or not, in fact it was described as Keynesian. Moreover, the interesting thing is that what they took to be Keynesian was not necessarily what Keynes would have taken to be Keynesian. As you know, and, I believe in the last article he ever wrote, which has been published posthumously in the *Economic*

Journal, he expressed great reservations about what was happening, about what some of his disciples were doing with his theories; he said there was much strength in these old ideas and that you must be careful not to carry some of the new ideas too far because you would destroy the system if you did. I have always thought it a great tragedy that Keynes did not live another twenty or thirty years because he was the only intellectual in the world, the only economist in the world, who had the intellectual influence that would have enabled him to have avoided some of the extravagances, some of the extreme measures, that were taken under the name of his theories.

BLAUG: Yes, what might have happened if Keynes had not died in 1946? We know that he had been worried even before the war about what might happen to prices if unemployment dropped below 10 per cent in 1937 or 1938. He might have been been more worried in the late '40s and '50s when the British economy reached a position of over full employment. Unemployment was as low as 1.5 to 2 per cent and there is every reason to think that he would have thought that this was as dangerous as setting off a possible wage-price inflation. What might have happened if he had lived?

FRIEDMAN: The crucial respect in which it would have made a difference if Keynes had lived longer was with respect to inflation. His disciples were the product of the 1930s. Inflation was the last thing in the world they were worried about. Deflation, depression all seemed to them the only important problems. Keynes, after all, was a product of the First World War and the post-war period. In his book on monetary reform, he chronicles the effect of these disastrous post-World War One inflations. He was just as strongly opposed to inflation as any hard gold bug you can imagine. He said in the *Monetary Reform* that the most effective way to destroy a nation is to destroy its currency. And he has a very eloquent statement along these lines. You can do it in a way which not one in a million persons can understand. That's what he says. (Maybe it's not a million, maybe it's ten millions.) Anyway, to go on, I have no doubt he would have been much more sensitive to the inflationary dangers that were implicit in the so-called 'Phillips Curve Approach' and the approach to economic management which said, 'Well, you can afford a little bit more inflation because that will have the good effect of reducing unemployment. And we don't have to worry about inflation because we know that that can be kept under control.' He wouldn't have taken that attitude at all; he would have been strongly opposed to it.

Similarly, I cannot believe, in line with all of his writings, that he would have been favourable to the kind of attempt at managing wages and prices in detail. In fact, one of the main virtues he saw in his own theory was that you could let the private market work with respect to individual prices, and individual wages and so on, provided the government provided the framework which would enable total demand to be adequate.

So his view was that government could play a role in setting the basic framework and then you can let the market do the rest. His disciples, some of his disciples, some of his followers who were very strong central planners, who saw this as a way in which they could justify having the government determine everything, would certainly not have gone along with him. He would have broken with them, I have no doubt of that.

On the other hand, there was another aspect of his thinking in which it wouldn't have mattered at all, in my opinion, if he had remained alive. And this had to do with his political philosophy and view. He was a paternalist, a believer in an élite. He thought the intellectual élite of people like himself, and so on, a Cambridge-educated élite, would be able to run the country for the benefit of the poor masses who did not understand what was going on. He was aristocratic fundamentally in his views, a carry-over from the nineteenth century in that respect. I may say I have a great admiration for him as an economist, but I differ with him profoundly on his political philosophy. I believe in democracy and I believe that you have to let people run the country, and not a self-elected élite that knows better than people what's good for them.

BLAUG: That brings us to the period of stagnation of the 1970s when, rightly or wrongly, many people thought Keynesian economics was totally irrelevant and indeed wrong. Just as they had thought in the '50s and '60s that the prosperity confirmed Keynes, stagnation refuted Keynes.

FRIEDMAN: The stagnation of the '70s did refute Keynes. It was a blatant contradiction to the predictions that his disciples drew from his theory. One after another of them had said that inflation cannot co-exist with unemployment. You can find quotation after quotation of that kind. But here you had a period in which inflation kept getting higher and higher and so did the level of unemployment. So it was a straightforward contradiction of a basic implication of the Keynesian view.

You know, in all scientific experiments you have crucial experiments, and a theory may be right ten times and it may have implications that are right, but if on a crucial element it is contradicted, that means that theory has to be replaced. And there was a very crucial element of the Keynesian theory as it had been developed by his disciples. And you couldn't have had a more dramatic contradiction of it.

BLAUG: In light of that contradiction, does anything in Keynesian economics endure or survive?

FRIEDMAN: In my opinion, if you mean by Keynesian economics the theory of *The General Theory*, essentially none of its substance survives. What survives is its language. We all of us use the Keynesian terminology. We all of us look at the problem in a different way, because of what Keynes did, but of the actual substantive theory nobody any longer believes in the sort of simple-minded propositions that were at the heart of Keynes's own theory. Nobody believes that what determines the interest rate is solely what is actual quantity of money in nominal terms. In the heyday of Keynes, a man teaching Keynes could stand before his students and say, 'Well, if you think the interest rate ought to be lower, all you have to do is to increase the quantity of money more rapidly.' Nobody can say that today. It's absurd. We all know that the way to make interest rates high is to increase the money rapidly. That produces inflation. That produces high interest rates. That's exactly the opposite of the conclusion that would have been drawn from a straightforward application of Keynesian doctrines.

Again, nobody anymore today says, 'All we have to do to keep unemployment down is to let inflation stay at about 3 per cent a year and that will give us 2 per cent unemployment', and so on. Nobody can say that any more.

BLAUG: This is, of course, Keynesian economics represented as a body of statements or propositions about the economy. But what about Keynesian economics as a set of ideas about economic policy?

FRIEDMAN: But the economic policy ideas followed directly from those propositions about the economy. Economic policy ideas were that all the government had to do was to spend and spend, and print and print. If there was any slightest sign of the economy flagging, according to simple Keynesian ideas, all the government had to do was to increase its spending or decrease taxes – either one would do from that point of view – and to make sure that interest rates were low enough, all you had to do was print money. Now, is there anybody who follows that policy now? I don't believe so. No government does and no respectable economist to my knowledge would support such a policy.

BLAUG: How could we then sum up the influence of Keynes, distinguishing perhaps, when talking about the influence, his influence on the shape of economic theory, his influence on ideas about economic policy and, lastly, his influence on the general intellectual climate of the last fifty years?

FRIEDMAN: I think his influence on economic theory is, on the whole, a very good one, not because the theory he proposed was right, but he taught us all to look at the problems through different lenses, developed a terminology that has turned out to be very useful to people like myself who never have accepted the basic elements of his theory. And he was the right kind of an economist as an economic scientist from my point of view.

So far as economic policy is concerned, I think that goes along with his influence on the general intellectual climate. In that respect, I think he has had a very bad influence, because he encouraged the tendency of the intellectual community to believe that: (a) the way to solve all problems was to have governments solve them; and (b) the way to have governments solve the problem was to put intellectuals in charge of it. In that respect, in promoting the notion that it was government you had to look to to solve the problems rather than the private activities of individuals – private voluntary activities; that compulsion was preferable in many cases to voluntary co-operation and that intellectuals had special claims to be the persons who turned the dials and pulled the levers of power – in those respects I think Keynes's influence was wholly bad.

*   *   *

Epilogue

Perhaps we can close with a statement from Keynes himself. The closing paragraph of *The General Theory* contains one of the most quoted statements that Keynes ever made:

> The ideas of economists and political philosophers, both when they are right and when they are wrong, are more powerful than is commonly understood. Indeed, the world is ruled by little else. Practical men, who believe themselves to be quite exempt from any intellectual influences, are usually the slaves of some defunct economist. Madmen in authority, who hear voices in the air, are distilling their frenzy from some academic scribbler of a few years back.

No doubt in making that statement, Keynes meant to include himself and we can only say that he was absolutely right.

Suggestions for Further Reading

The literature on Keynes and the General Theory is immense, but much of it is not suitable for beginning students in economics. However, everyone will benefit from M. Stewart, *Keynes and After* (London: Penguin Books, third edition, 1986 – avoid the earlier editions) and D. E. Moggridge, *Keynes* (London: Fontana paperback, 1976). For an accessible and iconoclastic collection of essays on the legacy of Keynes, see J. Burton, (ed.) *Keynes' General Theory: Fifty Years On* (London: Institute of Economic Affairs, 1986). Of all the commentators on Keynes, the greatest of them all, in my opinion, is Don Patinkin. For a sample of his interpretive powers, see his masterful entry on Keynes in *The New Palgrave. A Dictionary of Economics*, ed. J. Eatwell, M. Milgate and P. Newman (London: Macmillan, 1987), vol. 3, pp. 19–41. For further details on the Keynesian Revolution, see my 'Second Thoughts on the Keynesian Revolution', in *Economic Theories, True or False?* (Aldershot: Edward Elgar, 1990).

On Keynes's life, there is only one book: Robert Skidelsky, *John Maynard Keynes*, vol. 1, *Hopes Betrayed, 1883–1920*; vols 2/3 *The Economist as Prince, 1920–1946* (London: Macmillan, 1983, forthcoming). It is a fascinating and absorbing study of a man, his ideas and those of a whole era.

What of Keynes himself? *The General Theory* is, as I have said, a very tough book but to see how well Keynes could write when he stopped impressing his fellow academics, see the last chapter of *The General Theory*, chapter 24, entitled 'Concluding Notes on the Social Philosophy Towards Which the General Theory Might Lead'. It is only twelve pages long, but every sentence is quotable, and every other sentence denies one or another myth that has cluttered the reputation of Keynes.

Index of Names

Index of Subjects

Also by Mark Blaug

ECONOMIC THEORY IN RETROSPECT
THE METHODOLOGY OF ECONOMICS
GREAT ECONOMISTS BEFORE KEYNES
GREAT ECONOMISTS SINCE KEYNES
WHO'S WHO IN ECONOMICS
INTRODUCTION TO THE ECONOMICS OF EDUCATION
THE CAMBRIDGE REVOLUTION

JOHN MAYNARD KEYNES
Life, Ideas, Legacy